The Fre  Handbc

Toasts, Speeches and Responses

Yasha Beresiner

Lewis Masonic

About the Author

Yasha Beresiner was born in Turkey in 1940. His family emigrated to Israel in 1948 and he came to England for his primary education. He returned to Israel for military service in the parachute regiment (and married his sergeant Zmira in 1964). He qualified with a law degree from the Hebrew University of Jerusalem. In 1969, the family settled permanently in London. He was initiated into Freemasonry in 1975 and invited to join the Quatuor Coronati Lodge 2076, the premier Lodge of Masonic research, where he served as Master in 1998/9. He has been honoured with Grand Rank under the English (PGStB), Italian (PSGW) and Israeli (HonSGW) jurisdictions and was proclaimed the 2009 Blue Friar by this respected and eccentric USA Order. He is active in many Orders beyond the Craft.

His main interests outside of Freemasonry revolve around the City of London. He is a qualified City guide (red badge 2002) and editor of the association's quarterly magazine. In 2001/2, he served as Master of the ancient city livery company (est. 1628) The Worshipful Company of Makers of Playing Cards. He has written a total of ten books/booklets and has had a plethora of articles published worldwide. The greatest hobby he has is his seven grandchildren. He will be happy to make contact with his readers through his website — www.intercol.co.uk

First published 2009
Reprinted 2011

ISBN 978 0 85318 336 5

Published by Lewis Masonic

an imprint of Ian Allan Publishing Ltd, Hersham, Surrey KT12 4RG.
Printed by Ian Allan Printing Ltd, Hersham, Surrey KT12 4RG.

Code: 1107/A2

Visit the Ian Allan Publishing website at www.lewismasonic.com

CONTENT

By the same Author:

The Paper Tiger, (with Art Buchwald and U Ben-Yehuda). Eichenberger, 1968
Colombian Currency, Stanley Gibbons, 1973
The Story of Paper Money (with C Narberth), David and Charles, 1974
A Collectors Guide to Paper Money, Andre Deutsch, 1977
British County Maps, ACC, 1983
The Ortiz-Patiño Collection of Playing Cards, InterCol, 1995
Masonic Curiosities, ANZMRC, 1999
Royal Arch: The 4th Degree of the Antients, Supreme Grand Chapter of
    England, 2000
City of London – A Masonic Guide, Lewis Masonic, 2007
Masonically Speaking, Lewis Masonic, 2008

Dedication

This reprint of the booklet is dedicated with all my heart to Noah and Isaac, the two newest boys in the Beresiner dynasty.

Preface

I would like to re-iterate that it is a pleasure and honour to be asked by my colleague and friend, Yasha, to write the preface to his booklet on Masonic speeches. This little publication follows on his highly successful *Masonically Speaking* and, in many ways, complements the book. Here every Mason will be able to find and adapt a speech for every occasion in every order. As Brother Beresiner states in his introduction, anyone using the book needs some initiative in selecting, combining and most importantly, adapting the selected speeches to the circumstances in which he finds himself.

I have no doubt that every Freemason will find this an exceedingly useful booklet, well written and presented and I thank Yasha for the preview I had, which gave me an early opportunity to make use of some of his excellent stories.

Dr. John Wade, PPJGW (Yorks W R and Derbys)
Prestonian Lecturer 2009, London, June 2011

Introduction

Dear Reader,

This little volume, self-contained and published in its own right, can be seen as an addendum, a companion, to my *Masonically Speaking* published in 2008 and in which detailed guidelines are given for Masonic and other speech-making. Here I present actual speeches for those Masonic occasions where a speech may be required. Reference on 'how to' and practical instructions have been omitted and are included in the above titled booklet.

It is impossible to write a speech that would be universally acceptable to any speaker for any particular occasion. Clearly, the speeches presented here are not intended to be learnt verbatim. A speaker, in selecting any speech quoted, has to adapt, add and amend the text to suit and accommodate his specific needs, thus personalising and creating a text that will reflect his own feelings and sentiments relevant to the occasion. There is no substitute for personalising a speech.

To benefit from this booklet you will have to empathise with me. Use, so far as practicable, my words and mould them into the new shape that will finally satisfactorily reflect what you have to say. You have the obvious option of selecting stories and anecdotes from different speeches in order to compose your own unique speech. I have used considerable artistic licence, not least in the selected names of famous Freemasons, some of which are easily recognisable. Many of my comments may be exaggerated truths or amusing falsehoods. Historical references and dates, however, are accurate.

Some of the practices referred to and which apply to London may have minor variations in the Provinces.

Whilst the references are all to Craft events, with simple logic the speeches may easily be adapted to any of the Orders beyond the Craft. The notes preceding some of the speeches are intended as comments and reminders, rather than instructions.

I have decided to group separately the speeches given as 'toasts' from those that are 'responses'. It would have been as convenient to follow each toast by a response. There are also sections dedicated to speeches, presentations etc. which do not require response.

Timing is probably the most important aspect in the refinement of a speech. Where I have shown three dots . . . allow emphatic few seconds to pass by, before uttering the punch line.

Remember two golden rules: that brevity is the true secret of success and that you are here to have a good time.

Enjoy your food, the wine drinking, toasts and speeches.

Yasha Beresiner

Preamble

Masonic Wine Taking and Masonic Toasts

There appears to be more confusion with regard to 'wine taking' as opposed to 'toasting' than is necessary. These are two separate and distinct procedures.

The Wine Taking (or *'Taking Wine'*) is conducted during the meal, normally between the first and second courses. It is intended to acknowledge, effectively welcome, various brethren present at the festive board. It is, for all practical purposes, informal. It is the Worshipful Master's prerogative to decide on the frequency and sequence of Wine Takings. It is worth noting however, that the procedure, when uncontrolled, can become tedious.

Originally the Master took wine with his Wardens, with the Grand Officers present and all the brethren. Today the custom has expanded and it is recommended that no more than five risings take place. On Installation and initiation nights, the appropriate wine takings are a matter of courtesy. So it is on occasions when a brother celebrates a new honour. There is no breach of protocol in combining more than one item at any one rising.

The simple procedure for wine taking starts with the Wardens. The Worshipful Master sounds his gavel, and the Immediate Past Master or Director of Ceremonies enquire:

'Bro. Wardens, how do you report your respective Columns?'

The Senior Warden replies:
'All charged in the West, Worshipful Master.'

The Junior Warden replies:
'All charged in the South, Worshipful Master.'

The Immediate Past Master or Director of Ceremonies will state:

'Brethren, the Worshipful Master will be pleased to take wine with his Wardens.'

There then follow the other wine takings.

NOTES *The Director of Ceremonies should ensure that wine has been served and all glasses are filled.*

It is only the Master that gavels (as in lodge, the gavel never leaves the Master's hand)

There are no speeches, comment or fire following wine taking.

Both 'parties' to the wine taking stand to drink, whether a newly made brother or a Grand Officer, unless the Director of Ceremonies states, 'You may remain seated and the Master alone will stand.'

The Masonic Toasts, as opposed to wine taking, are a more formal part of the procedures at the festive board. I repeat, the gavel remains with the Master at all times. The Wardens reply to the Master's single knock. The Director of Ceremonies calls the brethren's attention to the Master. The Master or Director of Ceremonies announces the various toasts. The first responsibility of the Master at the completion of the meal, after the tables have been cleared and the dining room has been duly tyled, is to invite the

Chaplain to say Grace (see *Appendices E38*). The toasts may now start with the two traditional toasts to the Queen and the Grand Master, given without comment. (In very exceptional circumstances, such as recovery from illness or some important political or social event, very few suitable words may be added to the otherwise standard format.)

THE TOASTS

The Loyal Toast to The Queen

In some London Lodges the Wardens rise at the same time as the Master to honour the Toast. The toast is followed by 'fire' (see Appendix Item 37). There are no directives as to what constitutes correct 'fire'. The words 'Good Fire' are an alternative and preferable to 'Quick Fire'. It is sometime stated that 'with me' is preferable to 'from me' or that nothing more than 'Good Fire, brethren' need be said. The Master gavels, the Wardens respond and the Director of Ceremonies announces:

Brethren – pray silence for the Worshipful Master who will propose the loyal toast – upstanding brethren.

The Master now says:

Brethren, the first toast of the evening is to the Queen and the Craft. *(The 'Queen' is omitted from this toast in all Orders except for the Craft and Royal Arch)*

The brethren rise and drink. The Worshipful Master now continues with the 'fire'. The following is the sequence for the 'fire' as given in London and differs in rhythm and speed in different Provinces:

Good Fire, brethren, and take the time from me.

The Master or brother giving the toast marks time with his finger in the air and states out loud:

'P - - - - , L - - - , R - - - - , P - - - - , L - - - , R - - - - , P - - - - , L - - - , R - - - - , One, Two'

All now join and complete the triad *Three* with a clap and continue three times with three claps: *123, 123, 123.*

The Grand Master

NOTE *For the next toast the Master gavels for a second time. The Director of Ceremonies claims the brethren's attention. The Worshipful Master announces the second toast of the evening: (Each of the Orders beyond the Craft has its own Grand Master).*

Brethren, I give you the Toast to the Most Worshipful Grand Master:

His Royal Highness the Duke of Kent.

(Titles: GCMG, GCVO &c, are omitted.)

The 'fire' as described above follows the toast.

These two toasts, obviously without response, are obligatory and set apart from the remainder that follow.

The responses that follow the individual toasts have been separately listed in the section titled Responses.

1. Grand Lodge

Toast proposed to Grand Lodge

NOTE *When there are no Grand Officers present, the following toast is given without comment. The Master gavels. The Director of Ceremonies claims the brethren's attention. The Worshipful Master announces the next toast of the evening:*

Brethren, I give you the next Toast to:

The Most Worshipful Pro Grand Master:
Peter Geoffrey Lowndes;

The Right Worshipful Deputy Grand Master:
Jonathan Spence;

The Right Worshipful Assistant Grand Master:
David Kenneth Williamson

and the rest of the Grand Officers, Present and Past.

Brethren, please be upstanding.

The 'fire' is given following the toast.

Toast Proposed to the Grand Lodge, Grand Lodge Officers and/or Grand Officers

NOTES *If one or more Grand Officers are present, the Worshipful Master may give a brief speech after announcing the toast as detailed above. The Master is expected to invite a response by the most senior Grand Officer present. When referring to the Grand Officer, his Masonic rank is given in full, for example, Past Assistant Grand Director of Ceremonies and not abbreviated with initials alone e.g. PAGDC.*

Also **NOTE** *the difference between a Grand Lodge Officer, namely a Grand Officer holding active Grand Rank, normally for a limited period, and a Grand Officer who holds Past Grand Rank. In its simplest form the speech need be no more than:*

Brethren, I give you the next toast to:

The Most Worshipful Pro Grand Master:
Peter Geoffrey Lowndes;

The Right Worshipful Deputy Grand Master:
Jonathan Spence;

The Right Worshipful Assistant Grand Master:
David Kenneth Williamson

and the rest of the Grand Officers, Present and Past, a number of whom are present here with us this evening. It is always a delight to welcome them and I have much pleasure in coupling with this toast the name of Worshipful Brother Thomas Dunckerley, Past Assistant Grand Director of Ceremonies and I ask that you stand and drink their very good health.

Followed by 'fire'

Toast Proposed to the Grand Lodge Officers and/or Grand Officers

Brethren, I give you the next toast to:

The Most Worshipful Pro Grand Master:
Peter Geoffrey Lowndes;

The Right Worshipful Deputy Grand Master:
Jonathan Spence;

The Right Worshipful Assistant Grand Master:
David Kenneth Williamson

and the rest of the Grand Officers, Present and Past and before asking you to stand and drink a hearty toast, may I point out that we are honoured by the presence of several eminent and distinguished Grand Officers, and I have much pleasure in coupling with this toast the name of Worshipful Brother John Desaguliers, Past Assistant Grand

Director of Ceremonies, who will respond on their behalf.

Brethren, I would like to emphasise our collective awareness of the long history of the administration of our Craft by men of strength, ability and consequence. They have served the fraternity over the past three centuries. It is in their footsteps that Grand Officers tread today and in toasting them we secure the continuity of this long history and our wonderful traditions.

An ancient charge by the Master, which I would like here to repeat, began:

'Charge, brethren! Charge your glasses to the top,
My toast forbids the spilling of a drop.'

And concludes:

May unity, friendship, and brotherly love, ever distinguish the brethren of the Ancient Craft and their leaders.

I therefore ask that you stand and drink the very good health of our 'Leaders': Grand Lodge and its Officers.

Followed by 'fire'

Toast Proposed to A newly Appointed Grand Officer member of the Lodge

Brethren, I give you the next toast to:

The Most Worshipful Pro Grand Master:
Peter Geoffrey Lowndes;

The Right Worshipful Deputy Grand Master:
Jonathan Spence;

The Right Worshipful Assistant Grand Master:
David Kenneth Williamson

and the rest of the Grand Officers, Present and Past. Brethren, this important toast to the rulers of the Craft is often given without inviting a response. On this occasion, however, we can take great pride in our own Brother Tommy Cooper having recently been appointed a Past Assistant Grand Director of Ceremonies of the United Grand Lodge of England and I have very much pleasure, therefore, in coupling his name to this toast.

Bro Tommy, initiated in our Westminster Lodge No. 4518, in 1952, has been a tireless contributor to the welfare and fun of the lodge over the past decades. Every member will agree I know, that his preferment is truly well deserved. We wish him good luck and continued success, not least in his activities in our lodge.

I recall Tommy in his youth, as keen a member of the lodge as I had known, coming to me very excited by the fact that he had discovered an exceptional and infallible way of learning the ritual: 'All I do,' he said, 'is to have a recording of the ritual (naturally omitting the essential words) playing under my pillow every night as I go to sleep. It works like a dream,' he enthused. At the next meeting of the lodge I asked him how he was progressing with his new idea and he replied rather sadly, 'It is amazing, I have already learnt the first three degrees and the charge to the initiate almost word perfect . . . The problem is that I can only recite them whilst I am sleeping.'

We look forward to seeing him in our midst, always proud and smiling, for many years to come.

Brethren, I ask that you be upstanding to drink the

health of Worshipful Bro Tommy Cooper, our newly appointed Grand Officer.

Followed by 'fire'

2. Toast Proposed to The Masonic Charities
(normally given by the Charity Steward of the Lodge)

NOTE *This is a toast given when a Grand Officer, representative of a Masonic institution is present. He will normally be present for a specific purpose, such as launching of the Worshipful Master's appeal or to receive a donation.*

Brethren, among the Grand Officers present this evening, we have the great pleasure of welcoming Bro Dr William Dodd, Past Provincial Grand Chaplain and Chairman of the Royal Masonic Benevolent Institution, who is here with a specific purpose in mind and I will shortly invite him to respond to this toast.

Let me first, however, express our most sincere appreciation and congratulations on his exceptional achievements since his appointment. Freemasonry is essentially and practically a charitable organisation. Charity, that is, of both the heart and the pocket and in Bro Dodd we have a man who ideally symbolises those tenets of our fraternity. There is a well known parable about charity that can be repeated here.

A priest visiting his neighbouring parish on a Sunday morning was offered the content of the Charity collection as a gesture of welcome. On his return home he told his wife what had happened. 'The charity box was first presented to me,' said the priest, 'and I placed one pound in it. It then went around the whole of the congregation and was presented to me at the end. Would you believe,' said the incredulous priest to his wife, 'that the total content of the charity collection came to just the one pound I had put in?!' 'Well,' replied the wife, 'you should have put ten pounds in the charity box, shouldn't you!'

Brethren, we will always benefit to the same degree that we contribute. An old charge of the 19th century declares: *'May virtue ever direct our actions with respect to ourselves, justice to those with whom we deal, mercy, love and charity to all mankind.'* It stands as true a sentiment today as it will so long a Freemasonry is alive.

I ask you, brethren, to stand and drink the good health of our Bro Reverend Dr William Dodd'.

Followed by 'fire'

3. Metropolitan/Provincial Grand Lodge

Toast Proposed to the Metropolitan or Provincial Grand Master (in his absence)

NOTE   *Unlike the Grand Master, whose presence at a Lodge meeting is highly improbable, that of the Metropolitan or Provincial Grand Master is common at some meetings, especially those of Installed Masters Lodges or at the Installation meetings of a lodge. In such instances it would be expected for the Worshipful Master to add a few personal words of welcome to the toast. Should the Metropolitan or Provincial Grand Master not be present, the standard toast is given thus:*

Brethren, I give you the next toast to The Right Worshipful Metropolitan Grand Master, Brother Russell John Race, (or to The Right Worshipful Provincial Grand Master of Essex, Brother John Webb).

Followed by 'fire'

Toast Proposed to the Metropolitan or Provincial Grand Master (in his presence)

NOTE *In the presence of the Metropolitan or Provincial Grand Master the toast may be extended thus:*

Brethren, it gives me enormous pleasure to be able to couple this toast with the name of our Metropolitan Grand Master, R W Bro Russell Race, who has graced our meeting this afternoon and has joined our festive board his evening. We are delighted, Bro Russell, that in your very busy schedule you found time to dine with us now.

Every London member of the Craft is pursuing your progress as our recently appointed Metropolitan Grand Master, with keen interest and full encouragement. It is my particular honour to be able to express on behalf of us all our admiration and total support for your efforts. We so often drink your health in your absence that it becomes a great privilege to do so personally and face to face.

I now ask the brethren to stand and drink the very good health of the Right Worshipful Metropolitan Grand Master, Russell John Race.

Followed by 'fire'

Toast Proposed to the Metropolitan or Provincial Grand Lodge and/or its Officers

Brethren, we are honoured and delighted this evening to have in our midst a number of Metropolitan/Provincial Grand Officers and I am sure you all join me in warmly welcoming this handsome delegation. The toast I am about to propose has roots going back to the start of Freemasonry in the 18th century. Drinking, eating and toasting were an integral part of Masonic activity and in the exposure titled *Jachin and Boaz*, published in 1762, we read, that 'the Ceremony of drinking health (sic) among the Masons, takes up much of their time.'

The statement is followed by a whole page of Masonic toasts from which the Master selected several, after each one a bumper toast being drunk by the brethren. These publications disclosing the supposed secret practices of the Masons, though intended to attack Freemasonry, actually give us a wonderful insight into the activities of our forefathers.

I am sure, brethren, you will therefore happily join me in continuing a long tradition of toasting. Our Metropolitan/Provincial Officers work tirelessly for our benefit and each one of us has enjoyed the personal services of one or more of our active Metropolitan/Provincial Grand Officers at some time or other. They work non-stop. I know from experience the problems associated with such recurrent Masonic activity. Early in my Masonic career my wife complained that there I was, again on my way to another Masonic meeting. I picked up the summons that had just arrived and said, 'Look, it says here "By Command of the Worshipful Master". I have to obey.' 'I wish I was your Worshipful Master,' she retorted. I did not comment but cannot deny the fleeting thought that we change our Worshipful Master every year.

Thank you, brethren of Metropolitan/ Provincial Grand Lodge, for joining us this evening and may we have the continued pleasure of your presence in many meetings to come.

Brethren, I ask that you be upstanding and drink the health of Metropolitan/ Provincial Grand Lodge.

Followed by 'fire'

Toast Proposed to A Newly Appointed Metropolitan Grand Officer

Brethren, Bro Chevalier Ruspini, a long serving member of this lodge, was recently honoured by our Metropolitan Grand Master and appointed Past Metropolitan Grand Standard Bearer and I am happy, in your name, to recognise his well deserved preferment.

Brethren, London has for centuries held a very special place in the heart of English Freemasonry. The Craft was born within the City in 1717 and spread to the Provinces over the years. Whilst Provincial Grand Masters were appointed, no such appointment was seen as necessary in London and the Masons in the City enjoyed an exceptional status with direct responsibility to the Grand Master (instead of a Provincial Grand Master, as was the case throughout England). It is only in the last decade or so that this situation has changed and the formation of the Metropolitan Grand Lodge has now levelled out the administration of the Craft throughout the Nation. It was not an easy task and it is still an ongoing process. The brethren serving as the Administrators of our relatively new Metropolitan Grand Lodge, which now includes our Bro Ruspini amongst them, have serious responsibilities resting on their shoulders. As London Masons, we have witnessed their work and effort, which has assured our success and contributed so well to our needs and comforts.

In wishing our newly appointed Brother happiness and a long life, may I remind him that the best way to live longer is to stop doing everything that makes him want to live longer? We had the pleasure of dining together just some months ago and Bro Ruspini was disgusted by the inclusion of 'Ox Tongue Soup' on the menu. 'How on earth can anyone eat something that has been in an animal's mouth?' he commented . . . and went on to order an egg omelette.

Brethren, I ask that you stand and drink the continued good health and prosperity of our Bro Ruspini.

Followed by 'fire'

Toast Proposed to Newly Appointed Provincial Grand Officer

Brethren, Bros Elias Ashmole and Colonel Henry Mainwaring, long serving members of this lodge, were recently honoured by our Provincial Grand Master and appointed Past Provincial Grand Standard Bearer and Past Provincial Grand Director of Ceremonies, respectively. I am happy, in your name, to recognise their well deserved preferment.

There has always been an element of independence shown by Provincial Lodges toward London. Not long after the formation of Grand Lodge a 'Deputy Grand Master's Country Feast' (to distinguish it from the Grand Feast) was held regularly in the Counties and led to the annual appointment of Stewards. These Country Stewards formed themselves into Lodge No 540 in November 1789 and were given the privilege of wearing a special jewel pendent from a green ribbon. When, however, in 1795, they petitioned for the right to wear a green apron (analogous to the red apron of the Grand Stewards) they were refused. The heated arguments that followed, in which even the then Acting Grand Master, the Earl of Moira, got involved, were so fierce that at one stage Grand Lodge removed the privilege of the Country Stewards to even wear the special green-ribboned jewel, originally granted in 1789. The brethren concerned were so relieved to have their Jewel privilege restored, that they no longer pursued their quest for a green apron but the antagonisms proved fatal and the last Country Feast was held in 1798, Lodge No 540 closing its doors for ever in 1799.

Had things gone differently we may well have had this handsome couple appearing before us in resplendent green aprons.

This will undoubtedly be the first of many honours to follow and may I, on behalf of us all, wish Brothers Elias and Henry continued success and hard work and ask that you stand to drink their health with a hearty toast.

Followed by 'fire'

4. Toast Proposed to the Consecrating Officers of a New Lodge (by the Master/senior Lodge member)

NOTE *It is customary to grant Consecrating Officers Honorary Membership of the Lodge as part of the Consecrating ceremony.*

Brethren, we have enjoyed this evening – a historic event in the consecration of our new lodge. We must consider ourselves privileged and this afternoon's ceremony will no doubt remain imbedded in our memories and our hearts for the remainder of our lives. All the more so for the beautiful way and efficient manner in which the ceremony was conducted by our Consecrating Officers. They are certainly well deserving of the honorary membership in our Lodge.

You will all, no doubt, have consistently been aware of the antiquity of the ceremony, first promulgated by James Anderson as a postscript to his 1723 *Constitutions*. He claimed, without evidence, alas, that the 'manner of Constituting a New Lodge' was 'in accordance to the ancient usage of Masons.' All the ritual work appears to have been in the hands of the Grand Master and those assisting him, who, having 'solemnly constituted the Lodge' present the new Master to the Fellow Crafts assembled. It was a time when Freemasonry enjoyed only two degrees, that of Entered Apprentice and Fellow Craft or Master Mason – which explains why our present related ceremonies take place in the second degree. We have moved some way since the more simplistic days of the past.

In those early days, men of standing were encouraged to join and attain the Chair of the Lodge as soon as possible. In a military lodge in Portsmouth the brethren were delighted to have persuaded their Commander in Chief to join the Craft. At the initiation ceremony, the two deacons responsible for the Colonel's perambulations were ordinary soldiers in the unit. The secretary chose to record this historic event in the minutes as 'one of those rare occasions when the candidate was led around the lodge by his privates.'

I wish to express our most sincere thanks to our Consecrating Officers who conducted an elaborate ceremony with such dignity and competence. As for us, may I quote the old refrain 'May the foundation of every regular Lodge be solid, its building sure, and its members numerous and happy.'

Brethren, I ask that you charge your glasses and be upstanding to drink the good health of our Consecrating Officers.

Followed by fire'

5. Toast Proposed to the Visiting Grand Officer

Brethren, this important toast to the rulers of the Craft is normally taken without inviting a response. On this occasion, however, we have with us W Bro John Wilkes, Past Assistant Grand Director of Ceremonies, who happens to be our Visiting Grand Officer and I will therefore couple his name with this toast.

Brethren, from the start of our Masonic careers, we are made aware of the standing and importance of the rulers in the Craft. As we gain experience, the part played by Grand Officers in the running and betterment of the Craft becomes more apparent. And as we grow in seniority, our ambitions and efforts will often revolve in the emulation of those senior to us and the hope, one day, of achieving the high and respected office of a Grand Officer. These ambitions have been imbedded in the hearts of Freemasons through generations and our own Bro Wilkes . . . who believes in reincarnation . . . since he was a young frog – exemplifies all the qualities to be found in a brother of his standing. He wears his apron with dignity, he addresses us with knowledge and humility and we can all feel all the more confident for having our interests represented in the Grand Lodge by him.

Brethren, I ask that you be upstanding and drink the health of W Bro John Wilkes, our visiting Grand Officer.

Followed by 'fire'

6.   Worshipful Master

Toast Proposed to the Worshipful Master

Worshipful Master, distinguished brethren and brethren, I am delighted and honoured to be invited to give this important toast to our newly installed Master, W Bro Irving Berlin. I have known Irving since before his association with Freemasonry and I can therefore allow myself, I feel, to share some thoughts about him, with you. You may, if you so wish, allow me some artistic or speaker's licence. The information I have is reliable, because it was given to me by a brother, whose name, of course, I cannot disclose, but I can tell you his wife's name: it is <u>Mrs</u> Cecil de Mills.

Speaking of wives, Irving was telling me that after 40 years of marriage he felt that he and his wife were like the two sides of a coin: they just can't face each other . . . but they still stay together. His father had told him that if he ever wanted to get married he should not hesitate – if he got a good wife, he would be happy and if he got a bad one he would become a philosopher. The final true secret of his happy marriage is that he and his wife go out for a romantic dinner every week of the year; candlelit restaurant with good food and wine and soft music . . . She goes Tuesdays and he goes Fridays. Unlike so many women who inspire us to do great things and prevent us from achieving them . . . Irving's wife has been the muse behind his success in life.

Brethren, Irving is an asset to this lodge, both as a man of standing and a dedicated Freemason. We can take great pride in having elected him as our Master and look forward to the remainder of the year under his guidance.

I now ask that you stand a drink the good health of our Worshipful Master.

Followed by 'fire'

Toast Proposed to the Worshipful Master
(on Installation Night by the Immediate Past Master)

NOTES *On Installation night in London lodges it is customary, though not obligatory, to follow the toast to the Worshipful Master with the Master's song (see Appendix E item 40). In brief, the brethren should remain seated, as the singer perambulates whilst singing. He first approaches the Junior Warden after the first verse and then the Senior Warden with the second. The brethren stand and join in the last chorus*

> *as the singer approaches the Worshipful Master from the front and the two Wardens flank him (the WM) reaching his side in synchrony with the singer. At the end of the song, all the brethren lift their glasses high and call out 'Worshipful Master' before drinking his health. An impressive and often emotional ceremony.*

Brethren, as the immediate Past Master of the Lodge, it is my privilege to continue in the long-standing tradition of giving this toast to our Worshipful Master, Bro Malcolm Campbell.

Our forefathers showed considerable wisdom in creating this very special 'office' of Immediate Past Master. It places me in a unique position. I enjoy all the pleasures of a Master, now past the chair, and have none of the duties of the office. A little like being a grandfather: all the joys and none of the responsibilities. It also places me physically here at the top table, to the left of the Master. This is an excellent vantage point, allowing me to view and survey all that is happening around me and when, if necessary, guide the Master.

At our last meeting, after the initiation of Bro Daniel Mendoza, I had the pleasure of giving him a lift home and asked him about his impressions of the ceremony. He said that the most impressive part was when the blindfold was taken off and the awesome sight of the senior brethren sitting in the East slowly came into focus. 'Who was the brother with all the dark blue and gold braid immediately to the left?' he asked. 'That,' I said solemnly, 'is the senior most Grand Officer present in the Lodge.' 'What about you, sitting on the right, as I faced you?' enquired Daniel. 'Well, I am the Immediate Past Master and the most recent senior member of the Lodge.' 'So what about the guy in the middle straight in front of me?' ventured our newly made Mason.

'He is undoubtedly the most important man in the room,' I said. 'He is the Worshipful Master.' 'If he is so important,' said Daniel, 'why did you and the others keep interrupting him all evening?'

Worshipful Master, the Lodge has bestowed on you the highest honour it has in its power to confer on one of its members and we look forward and wish you a splendid year in office. You follow on long-standing traditions, which in the early days of Freemasonry had no ceremony involved. Following the formation of Grand Lodge in 1717 there was no procedure recorded for the installation of a Master. It was only in 1722 that the Duke of Wharton, our sixth and rather controversial Grand Master, instituted '*The Manner of Constituting a New Lodge*' which incorporated the Installation of the Master without fuss or ceremony, merely sitting him in the Master's chair. It wasn't until 1827 that the final and standardised practices you experienced in lodge today were finally established.

It is our earnest hope that you, as our new Master, enjoyed the dignified ceremony and its significance and that you appreciate the duties and responsibilities you now bear on our behalf. We wish you, foremost, a happy year as Worshipful Master and feel confident that our lodge will flourish and prosper in the coming year under your wise guidance.

Brethren, I would ask that you stand and drink the good health of W Bro Malcolm Campbell, Worshipful Master.

Followed by 'fire'

Toast Proposed to the Worshipful Master
(on other than Installation Night)

Brethren, I have once more the pleasure and privilege of inviting you to toast our Worshipful Master, now well into his stride leading our lodge forward in its continued path of success. Unlike the political leader who proclaimed to the throng of the followers gathered around him: 'Just recently we were on the very verge of the precipice . . . Now we can take a bold step forward!'

The Master of a lodge, brethren, does not only act on behalf of the Lodge but he also embodies and represents every single member of the lodge. Our Master's dignity in the fulfilment of his duties reflects our own dignity. His spoken words echo our thoughts and sentiments. In these aspects of his duties, our Master has, to date, fulfilled his obligations with admirable success.

We can take pride and congratulate him on his labours and I now invite you to join me in drinking a hearty toast to Bro William Hogarth, our Worshipful Master.

Followed by 'fire'

Toast Proposed to the Worshipful Master
(when a Past Master)

Brethren, I have the great pleasure of proposing this toast to our well experienced Master on his second rotation, so to speak. Bro George Alexander has generously agreed to serve a second time in order to fill in a needed gap and we are all grateful to him for again taking on the duties of Worshipful Master of the Lodge.

Bro Alexander is well known and his experience will serve him and us well. We have heard him in action both within the confines of the Lodge and at the festive board. He is an accomplished speaker. As our new Master, we will be hearing him often in the coming year and he will not need to be reminded of Baron Montesquieu's famed quote that so many speakers want to convey depth but they only give us length. I cannot remember the name of the famous philosopher that said, 'Speech is the faculty given to man to conceal his thoughts.' I for one look forward to Brother Alexander's words of wisdom at our forthcoming meetings.

Brethren, there are great advantages to us having a Master of the calibre of Bro Alexander leading us through the next year. His competence means that we shall be represented with knowledge and dignity wherever he visits and I have no doubt we will enjoy other aspects of his experience during the course of the year that he will serve us.

The toast I am about to propose, brethren, has long-standing traditions that take us back to the famous *Schaw Statutes* first issued in Edinburgh in 1598 and which regulated, for the first time, the activities of the Masonic Lodges in Scotland. They laid precise rules for the 'banquets' that were to be provided, or paid for, by the Apprentices at their admission into the lodge and by the Fellows of the Crafts, when promoted.

In these early days in Scotland, the activities of working stone masons somehow combined with those of speculative ones, namely those who did not belong to the stone masons' trade. The presence of non-masons in operative lodges is manifest in a record of the Lodge of Aberdeen, which in 1670 required non-operative apprentices to provide, in addition to their entry money, a dinner with a 'speaking pint', whilst operative apprentices were admitted for lower fees, though they still had to provide refreshment. In England too, when Elias Ashmole visited the Masons Company in London in March 1682, he recorded in his diary that 'the noble dinner attended was given at the expense of the new accepted masons . . .' (What Ashmole was actually doing at the London Masons Company in 1682, is another story and remains a mystery.)

So you see, brethren, in asking you to stand and drink the health of our Worshipful Master, I take you back to traditions at the very beginning of Freemasonry as we understand and practise it today.

Please be upstanding and drink the excellent health of our Master, Worshipful, Brother George Alexander.

Followed by 'fire'

7. Toast Proposed to the Master Elect

Bro Nathan Rothschild, may I be the first to formally congratulate you on your election this evening as the next Master of this respected Lodge. We all look forward to your installation at our next meeting. Your progress through the lodge offices and your general interest in lodge affairs has been exemplary and I am confident that we will all enjoy the year of your Mastership. You have to be patient just a few more months during which time I look forward to your continued support and enthusiasm.

Bro Nathan's enthusiasm, brethren, is reflected in his high education and life achievements to date. He received his several degree from the Hebrew University in Jerusalem. I recall, totally incidentally, on a visit to the university having to go to the little boy's room and as I stood there, on the wall facing me was an enamelled plaque that read 'The future of the Jewish people is in your hands'.

Bro Nathan made his fortune in Manchester and later in London. Here the family Banking Empire was set up. In competition with world banks . . . he witnessed the Japanese Origami Bank fold and the Sumo Bank go belly up while his own businesses prospered. His contributions to the welfare of his fellow men are well recorded.

In asking you to stand to drink this toast to our Master elect, I would like to point out that the word 'toast' in the sense of 'drinking of health' did not make its appearance in the English language until about 1700. The earliest term we have for the equivalent of 'toasting' is the word 'pledge', conveying an expression of goodwill and friendship, and can be traced to 1546. Shakespeare in 1596 uses the words 'A Health' to mean the same thing.

So I ask that you stand and with this toast, pledge a health to our Master Elect, Bro Nathan Rothschild.

Followed by 'fire'

8. Toast Proposed to the Founders, Past Masters and Officers of the Lodge (traditionally given by the most junior member of the Lodge)

Worshipful Master, Past Masters and Officers of the Lodge, it is natural, I suppose, for me to be nervous on this occasion, the first occasion that I have of speaking at the festive board. I took the good advice of those whom I now address and remember that I am surrounded by friends and brethren who wish me well. That makes me feel much better.

Brethren, when I was initiated/passed/raised only a few months ago, I was warned that I will be invited to give this toast and I am truly very happy to do so. I have been observing the senior brethren of the lodge and I prepared a speech many months ago and have carried a copy of it in my pocket to every single meeting, waiting to be called upon. At last, I have been called upon . . . and left the speech at home!

Nonetheless, I remain aware of my sentiments: I feel that all of us in the lodge greatly benefit by the collective wisdom of its Past Masters and Officers under the direction of the Worshipful Master. We, the younger members, have great respect for you all and we appreciate your efforts and guidance in these, our early and formative years in Freemasonry. We are all ambitious to attain the ladder in the lodge and when we do so, we will do well to emulate the existing Officers in the quality and excellence of their work.

Thank you, brethren, for inviting me to propose this toast to the Past Masters and Officers of the lodge and I ask the brethren to stand and drink their good health.

Followed by 'fire'

9. Toast Proposed to the Initiate
   (by a Senior and competent member of the Lodge)

NOTES *Following his initiation, the candidate becomes a fully-fledged member of the lodge and is no longer a 'candidate' or 'initiate'. This is genuinely an important toast as it will constitute the new member's introduction to our fraternity. The toast needs to be delivered fluently and with confidence, welcoming him as 'one of us' in simple and clear terms. The*

newly made brother is bound to be somewhat
overwhelmed if not bewildered by the earlier
proceedings of his initiation.

Bro Winston Churchill, it is my very pleasant duty, on behalf of every member of the Studholme Lodge, indeed on behalf of Freemasons spread through the world, to welcome you into the midst of our very special fraternity. You will have been able to gain just a glimpse of the antiquity and depth of our Society during the ceremony of your initiation and I would like you to bear in mind that you have been treading in the footsteps of great men before you. For three hundred years and more, members of the British Royal family and the European Monarchies, Presidents of the United States of America and world politicians, historians, artists, musicians, actors, sportsmen, scientists and many others, with names you will readily recognise, have experienced and enjoyed the exact same ceremony that you went through this afternoon.

I have no doubt that you have many questions and I am confident, with time, they will all be answered. You will soon discover, if you have not already done so to some extent, the unjustified criticism directed at Freemasonry as a secret society. You will find that there are no secrets in Freemasonry beyond words and signs leading from one degree to the next. (Even those secrets are intended to protect new Masons from finding out details of their future advancement and are not directed toward the outside world.) The one and only true secret which will now reveal itself to you is the true and sincere brotherhood shared by the brethren of the society. It can only be discovered after one joins our organisation, as you have done today. I also have no doubt you will enjoy the antiquity of the organisation. When Freemasonry was formed as an organised body in June 1717, initiation ceremonies were performed in coffee houses, inns and taverns. The tracing board, now part of the furniture of the lodge, was physically drawn on the floor by the Tyler of the lodge. Among the duties of the newly initiated brother was his responsibility to wipe clean, with a mop and pail, the design which may otherwise be revealed to non-Masons. It was also the newly initiated member's responsibility to cover the cost of the dinner for the brethren. I have no doubt you will be glad to hear that this no longer applies.

Bro Winston, we welcome you with open arms and open hearts into our midst. You are now a full member of the lodge and can enjoy all the privileges which so satisfy the soul and spirit of each one of us. We trust you will duly progress through the future ceremonies and soon join us as a fully-fledged Master Mason. Meanwhile, enjoy your newly acquired friendships and we look forward to seeing you in our midst at our future meetings.

Brethren, I ask that you all stand and drink the good health of our new member, Bro Winston Churchill.

Followed by 'fire'

10 Toast Proposed to a Newly Elected Honorary Member (by Senior member of the Lodge)

Worshipful Master and brethren, thank you Worshipful Master, for asking me to propose this toast to our esteemed Brother Arthur Sullivan, who has served this lodge so well for so many years. Honorary membership, brethren, ironically brings with it some disadvantages as well as great privileges. The privileges are obvious in the standing, the very special standing, of the brother concerned as an outstanding member of the lodge, honoured by his peers and friends with special commendation. He does, however, also lose some of his rights. He is no longer able to vote or influence the lodge other than through his wise counsel and experience and will need to step down from the committees where he may have previously held office.

Bro Arthur has always been a great traveller and he may now find more time for his trips abroad. He always takes his apron with him in anticipation of some Masonic meeting or other that he may be invited to. On his last trip to South Africa he was stopped by the Johannesburg custom officials and asked to open his luggage. There on the top of his clothes lay his resplendent apron. The custom officer looked Arthur straight in the eye and said: 'Pass – free and of good report.'

Brethren, it is as great an honour to our lodge to have Bro Arthur as an Honorary Member as, I hope it is for him to be elected one, and I invite you to stand and drink the very good health of our newly elected Honorary Member, Worshipful Bro Arthur Sullivan.

Followed by 'fire'

11. Toast Proposed to a Joining Member
(by a Senior member of the Lodge)

Worshipful Master, thank you for inviting me to give this welcoming toast to our new joining member.

Brethren, many of you will already know Bro Bob

Monkhouse from his frequent attendance at our meetings and festive boards and we have enjoyed his company and his humour over the years. Unlike a new initiate, Bro Bob brings with him experience and knowledge of our Craft and we can look to him for advice and support. I am confident he will easily enter the flow of our lodge activities and support us in all matters.

There is a well knowing saying that some people create happiness wherever they go, others . . . whenever they leave and Bob certainly belongs to the former group. He is a genuinely clean cut man, not drinking excessively, eating with moderation and never gambles . . . Not since 7 July 1977 when he woke up and noticed that it was exactly 7 minutes past 7 am. This was much too much of a coincidence and Bob felt, contrary to his normal inclination for a small flutter, that there was some message in all the 7s of the day. He placed a bet of £7,777 and 77 pence on horse number 7 at the 7 o'clock race that evening. He should not have been surprised to find that the horse came in . . . seventh. He has not gambled since. Brethren, I suggest that Bro Bob's popularity is universal and I ask you to be upstanding and drink to the health of our new Joining member, Bro Bob Monkhouse.

Followed by 'fire'

12 Visitors and Guests

Toast Proposed to the Visitors and Guests

Brethren, I received a telephone call from our Worshipful Master yesterday who said that he wanted a responsible brother to give this important toast to the visitors. 'I want someone who has an element of wisdom and intelligence, with a tinge of appropriate sense of humour as well as someone who looks good and dignified on his feet.' He went on. 'Sadly, all of the brethren I have approached are otherwise engaged . . . so I find myself without choice and hope that you can help me out.'

I am delighted to comply and thank the Master for this opportunity to welcome our many visitors and guests present here this evening.

Bro guests, you are almost welcome here . . . I am sorry, brethren. I will start again: . . . Bro guests you are <u>all</u> . . . <u>most</u> welcome here this evening at our festive board and we hope you enjoyed the ceremony this afternoon. You will appreciate, brethren, that there is a distinct difference between a guest and a visitor, well exemplified when the opportunity arises to attend Wormwood scrubs, Holloway Prison or any other similar establishment. At the end of the allotted time period the visitors leave . . . whilst the guests stay behind. For the record a brother is a visitor to the lodge and a guest at the festive board and it is with sincere sentiments that we welcome you all.

The long tradition of visiting was less complex in the olden days. The dates of Masonic meetings were published in newspapers with the name of the tavern or coffee house where the meeting was to take place. A brother could attend and once vouched for, take part in the evening's proceedings. Sadly, attendance books and vouchsafing for a brother became necessary in the 1730s, as a result of the publication of Samuel Prichard's *Masonry Dissected,* which gave instruction on how to gain admittance into a lodge. It was to protect the brethren from unscrupulous persons attempting to gain access to the lodge charity that precautions had to be taken in admitting strangers into the lodge.

Nonetheless, visiting has continued as an important, friendly and warm tradition in all Lodges, not least the 'thematic' ones. The Bank of England Lodge, however, is having its problems in the present economic climate. As a visitor I was listening to two of the brethren talking and one said, 'We are looking for a new bank manager.' 'I thought you had employed a new bank manager just two weeks ago,' said the other. 'Yes, we did,' replied the first. 'He is the one we are looking for.' Brethren, it is quite amazing how far spread Freemasonry is. All quarters of the globe enjoy and practice the ritual in one form or another. A small group of Freemasons on a safari got lost in the wild jungles of Africa and were captured by a tribe of cannibals. Before they had the chance to realise what was going on they found themselves in a huge cauldron of boiling water. Suddenly one of the Masons noticed the chief cannibal giving the first degree sign. Excitedly, he shouted out: 'We are brothers! Please help us!' The chief approached the boiling pot slowly, paper and pen in hand and asked: 'What Lodge you belong to?' 'Magnus Carter . . . Please get us out of here,' came the hurried reply. A note was made and then the chief asked 'What number?' '1371 . . . Will you please help us?' The number was written down and the next question was: 'What is your rank?' 'For God's sake!' screamed the Mason. 'We are boiling alive! . . . Why are you asking all these questions?!' 'We need the information,' replied the chief cannibal, 'for our dinner menu.'

Brethren of the lodge, please be upstanding and drink the good health of our visitors and guests.

Followed by 'fire'

Toast Proposed to the Visiting Speaker
(by a selected Brother academically inclined)

Worshipful Master and brethren, we have been handsomely entertained in the lodge this afternoon by Bro Alfred Marks, to whom I am delighted to address this toast. It was the simplistic and very clear delivery of a relatively complex subject that was much appreciated. It brings to mind that Alexander Dumas once expressed surprise at how intelligent children were, and how stupid men can be. He came to the conclusion that it must be education that does it! I remember my 8-year-old son returning home from school after attending a well advertised lecture by a well known speaker. 'So what did the man have to say?' I asked with genuine interest. 'I don't know,' replied my son. 'You were not listening, were you?' I half-scolded him. 'I promise I was listening all the time, Dad,' replied my son, 'but the speaker never told us what he was talking about.'

Lecturing, brethren, is an old and established tradition in Masonic lodges and the minutes of the Lodge of Friendship, now No 6, take us back to 13 March 1738 where there is a record of a lecture on 'Education' by a Brother Clare 'after which the brethren drank to his Health and return'd him Thanks for his Instructive Lecture'. Those brethren who have through the centuries dedicated their time and effort in order to assist with our own Masonic education are to be appreciated and admired. In earlier days time did not seem to have been of essence. Laurence Dermott is reported to have put his listeners to sleep with a three hour rendition in the Antients Grand Lodge.

We are all the more grateful, therefore, Bro speaker for the compactness and duration of your presentation. It is a pleasant change from those occasions where the lecture is long finished but the speaker keeps talking!

It is not always easy for us to appreciate the amount of work involved in the preparation of a short talk, especially when it is delivered with such apparent ease and aplomb. His selected subject has been of the greatest interest and I know I speak on behalf of us all, members of the lodge and visitors, when I thank Brother Alfred for taking time to visit us here and impart, with such panache and fluency, his excellent lecture. The result is true profit and pure pleasure and we have certainly made our daily advancement in Masonic knowledge, this afternoon.

Brethren, please be upstanding to drink the good health of our guest speaker, Bro Alfred Marks.

Followed by 'fire'

Toast Proposed to a Visiting Demonstration Team

Worshipful Master and brethren

The demonstration that we witnessed this afternoon in lodge was a delight and pleasure, and it is my privilege now to thank the brethren of the Demonstration Team for their superb effort.

We are used to enjoy frequent performances of the various degrees and the installation ceremony through the course of the year. To be present at a demonstration of the quality and interest that we were privileged to attend this afternoon is a breath of fresh air. It is, I feel, the confidence with which the team performed that was particularly impressive, moderated by the modesty they have shown in the conversations we had at the bar before dinner. You know brethren, it is easy to be humble when you are successful, as our demonstrating team definitely are . . . The trick, they say, is to be arrogant when you are a complete flop! They have left an impression in our minds that we will long remember. I must admit, I have been having some problems with my memory, and when I went to my doctor about it . . . he made me pay in advance. I was forgetting the names of good friends and colleagues I had known for years. I did console myself that I could recall clearly the names of my enemies, which was far more useful. There is, of course, an important difference between not thinking of someone and forgetting him completely.

Brethren of the demonstration team, we will certainly not forget you and your performance, for a long time to come.

We, members of the lodge and the guests present alike, appreciate the many hours of practice that it takes to prepare for a presentation of the calibre we enjoyed this afternoon and I would ask that you all charge your glasses, stand and drink the health of the members of the Demonstration Team.

Followed by 'fire'

Toast Proposed to the Visitors from Foreign Jurisdictions

Brethren, whilst we frequently enjoy the presence of individual brethren from other lodges, it is not often that a delegation from overseas visits us and I am delighted to welcome the small party of brethren from Denmark.

We are very pleased that they selected our lodge for their visit this afternoon. It is a wonderful reminder of the universality of Freemasonry and a symbol of this amazing fraternity, that whilst we do not share a language, it has still been so easy to communicate with genuine brotherly love and affection. Unlike America and England, two great nations divided by a common language. You might have expected, brethren, that our differences would have led to silence, but quite the contrary is true and it has been a pleasure to observe animated exchanges and sharing of views. Not that there is anything wrong with silence or with having nothing to say . . . as long as you do not insist on saying it.

We trust that the Danish brethren will take home with them memories of an interesting and, most importantly, a truly friendly afternoon. Brethren from Denmark, on your return home, please convey the fraternal greetings of the Worshipful Master and brethren of our lodge and we hope that we will meet again, within this remarkable universal Masonic circuit.

Brethren of the lodge and guests of the English Constitution, I ask that you stand to drink the health of our Danish visiting brethren.

Followed by 'fire'

13. Toast Proposed to The Ladies

Mr President, Madame President, Ladies, Gentlemen and brethren, it is my great privilege this evening, Elizabeth (*addressing the Lady President*), to give this toast to you, our guest of honour, and to the other Ladies present here with us. The White Table is one of the great traditions in Freemasonry and a wonderful opportunity for us members of the lodge to get together with our respective ladies and friends. I must admit that I found preparing this speech to the ladies very difficult indeed. It is the matter of sincerity and the limited number of words in the English language that makes it so difficult. I would love to be able to express myself as briefly and clearly as the sign at our local jeweller's shop that says: 'Give her something to wrap around her little finger besides you.' Or my accountant, above whose desk is the large statement: 'No such thing as petty cash.'

How do I go about expressing our honest and genuine appreciation at your presence here, ladies, without relying on classical clichés that have been repeated in speeches again and again? What alternative words can we use to express the true sense of pride we feel at the grace and beauty that surrounds us? What can I say, on behalf of us all gentlemen present, other than 'Thank you, we love you and we appreciate you' without bordering on being patronising? You see my difficulty, ladies? . . . So I have decided to say none of this.

Instead, I will admit that we, as Freemasons, are a sentimental institution. We are not shy or ashamed of being sentimental. We genuinely and openly express brotherly love and affection and we practise it. We praise and support each other with a genuine heart and we see ourselves as an integral part of a big family. It is in this ambience and context that we welcome you amongst us and hope that you have enjoyed your evening as much as we have enjoyed your company.

We never forget how important you are to us, ladies. You know what they say: 'Behind every successful man there is . . . a surprised mother in law' and you know we will do anything for you. I remember as a legal student attending a court case where the judge asked the defendant

'Why did you rob the same shop three times?' The culprit replied, 'I only stole a dress for my wife, my Lord, and she made me change it twice.'

Finally, talking of ladies, I cannot but mention my dear departed dad, such a good friend and a brother, whose special fondness for the fairer sex remained unabated to his dying day. I will not cause offence, I know, when I tell you truthfully of his escapade on his 75th birthday. He rushed through the doors of the local catholic church exclaiming, 'Father, father. I need to confess.' 'Yes,' replied the sympathetic priest. 'It is my 75th birthday today and I celebrated by making love to a 25-year-old lady and—' 'Just a moment!' interrupted the priest. 'I recognise you. You are a member of the Jewish community. I am a catholic priest, why are you telling _me_?' 'Why am I telling you?' my dad replied. 'I am telling everybody!'

I will now ask all the gentlemen to stand and drink the health of our delightful ladies.

No 'fire'

14. Toast Proposed to The Lodge (on Anniversary)

NOTE   _Many Lodges publish a booklet or a more substantial volume for their anniversary. Mention of it should be made if a copy is presented to those attending._

Worshipful Master and brethren, you honour me on this auspicious occasion by inviting me to give this important toast to the lodge on its centenary. I remain aware of my responsibilities, speaking on behalf of so many guests here this evening, and know that I convey the great pleasure that we all have in being with you and to thank you for a splendid evening, so well organised in the lodge and so delightfully complemented by this delicious festive board.

Brethren, 100 years is a heavy chunk of history by any standards. As Freemasons, we can take great pride in the continuity of our institution, where many others have fallen by the wayside, because of the strength and devotion of individual members in lodges like this one. (*If applicable:* Your wonderful History published today and handed to us all is evidence of your perseverance and success.) The harmony and well-being of the lodge is reflected in the warm and friendly atmosphere of this evening. How wise of our forefathers to forbid from the start any religious or political discussion. It offers us the opportunity to discuss subjects of mutual interest without fear of creating tension . . . family, music and literature. My local amateur theatre group ambitiously decided to perform Shakespeare's Romeo & Juliet. It was well supported but sadly the comments that followed were far from complimentary. It did, however, make the local newspaper, in which the entertainment critic of the *Hendon Times* wrote: 'On Saturday last the members of our Amateur Dramatic Society staged Romeo & Juliet to a full house. The only benefit I can think of, which can now be achieved as a result of this performance is to finally establish whether Shakespeare or Bacon was the true author of the play. All that needs to be done is for their graves to be opened up and see which one turned over last Saturday night.'

Freemasonry, through its history, has suffered criticism and attacks from the outset: religious Papal Bulls in the early 18th century, anti-Masonic publications at repeated intervals, endeavours to have us banned and even physical imprisonment of Masons, for no other reason than their being members of the fraternity. We have survived because lodges like this one have persevered through good times and bad and have reached this day intact and proud and without disruption to their regular meetings.

I feel, brethren, on this very special occasion that it would be appropriate for all of us guests present, to stand and drink the very good health of the lodge on their special anniversary.

Followed by 'fire'

RESPONSES

15. Grand Officer

Response by a Grand Officer o/b of Grand Lodge

NOTE   *Grand Officers at this level of their Masonic careers will be well experienced and it would be presumptuous to suggest a suitable speech. The following guidelines, however, may be of assistance:*

Normally a single response by the senior-most Grand Officer present is expected.

The senior Grand Officer concerned may, of course, secede and allow a colleague to respond.

As the first speaker, the Grand Officer should remain aware of what speakers who follow may wish to say.

Grand Lodge business will be of interest to all brethren present.

The Royal Arch is a suitable subject for a Grand Officer to raise.

Congratulations to brethren going through the degrees or the newly Installed Master are customary.

Response by the Newly appointed Grand Officer member of the Lodge

Worshipful Master and brethren, it is a true honour for me to be able to stand before you with great pride as a newly appointed member of our Grand Lodge. I wish to thank you in person for your encouragement and instruction through my years as a member of this lodge, culminating in the honour of a Past Grand Officer bestowed on me by our Grand Master. I am pleased to inform all and sundry, particularly some of my colleagues from foreign jurisdictions, that the word 'past' in this context in England does not mean 'dead'!

Unlike Scottish, Irish and many foreign Constitutions, in England we differentiate between a *Grand Officer,* the rank to which I have been appointed, and a *Grand Lodge Officer,* who is a brother appointed to active office in Grand Lodge. Such brethren who have completed their term of service will retain their original rank with the word 'past' now preceding their title. In England alone it was decided some 150 years ago that because it would be impossible to provide active Office in Grand Lodge to all brethren who may have qualified for such promotion, the Grand Master would have the power to confer a Past Grand Rank on deserving brethren, in recognition of their services to the Craft. That is in spite of their not having served any office in Grand Lodge. Such Past Grand Officers, including myself, brethren, constitute the vast majority of Grand Officers.

On a personal note, I feel great pride in having attained this Grand Rank in our remarkable institution and am especially aware of my new status as I stand and speak to you to convey the greetings of Grand Lodge. I keep recalling, however, the immortal words of our Prime Minister, being introduced to a somewhat diffident and timid ambassador saying to him: 'Please do not be so modest . . . you are not as important as you think you are!'

Thank you, Worshipful Master and brethren, for your warm, welcome toast and I promise to represent you well and have you constantly in my thoughts as I enjoy my time in the very privileged position I find myself in. Thank you.

16. Response by a Grand Officer representative of a Masonic Institution

Worshipful Master and brethren, I am with you this evening because I have the great pleasure of assisting with the launching of your Master's selected charity, the RMBI, of which I have the great honour to be Chairman. (*At this stage the brother concerned will be able to give his rendition of the charity he represents.*)

You will have appreciated my spontaneous off-the-cuff speech, which I trust you found appropriate, as it was well rehearsed!

Brethren, it has been my good fortune to visit numerous lodges throughout the country and I will readily admit that this has been among the most pleasant evenings I have had the chance to attend. Thank you for your many generosities, in the lodge and here at this exceptional festive board. Your relentless charitable work has been of great help, well received and faithfully applied and I thank you, on behalf of the very many beneficiaries, for your generosity.

Thank you, Worshipful Master and brethren.

17. Response by a Metropolitan or Provincial Grand Officer o/b of Metropolitan or Provincial Grand Lodge

Worshipful Master and brethren, we are delighted to have been present at your proceeding in the lodge this afternoon and thank you for your kind and generous hospitality at the festive board. It is a delight to see a lodge happy and communicating happiness, as you have done today.

I think we are particularly impressed by the perfect timing of all your proceedings. It seems that there is some logic in the truth that time is what prevents everything from happening all at once. This also proved true when we arrived here this afternoon. The moment we entered the Lodge, your efficient Director of Ceremonies welcomed us warmly, took us aside . . . and left us there.

I feel confident that I speak on behalf of all my colleagues present with me, the delegation from the Metropolitan/Provincial Office, when I express our pride at having your lodge in London/the Province. You and your brethren, Worshipful Master, have been overt and great supporters of London/the Province and its activities manifest in the number of Metropolitan/Provincial Grand Officers you have as members of the lodge. We appreciate, remain aware and thank you for the strength of your support.

May you long continue with your success and representation of London/our Province in your many Masonic activities.

Thank you, Worshipful Master and brethren.

18. Response by the Consecrating Officer o/b of Consecrating Team

Worshipful Master and brethren, on behalf of the whole of the consecrating team, may I congratulate you first, Worshipful Master on the role you will be playing in leading this band of distinguished brethren, the founder members of this new and latest lodge to join our great fraternity under the jurisdiction of the United Grand Lodge of England.

We, as representatives of Grand Lodge, welcome you wholeheartedly and wish the lodge success and affluence in the future. May you always shine as a beacon of hope and an example of true brotherly love in a world that is not always in a happy state of affairs. Just recently my colleague was grumbling at the disasters that had taken place in his life: 'We are just three months into the new year,' he said, 'and in January my wife left me, in February my business went bust and in March my young unmarried daughter got pregnant . . . What can be worse?' he asked in exasperation. I could not withhold my response: 'April?' I suggested sheepishly.

No such sad stories with you, Worshipful Master and brethren. May you prosper from month to month and for many years to come. It has been our privilege this afternoon to conduct the ceremony of consecration in accordance with ancient custom and we have done so with a sense of special privilege in bringing forth a lodge whose membership is particularly distinguished and whose future is bright and promising.

Thank you, brethren.

19. Response by the Visiting Grand Officer or Visiting Officer

NOTES *Grand Lodge official business has often got to be incorporated into this speech.*

Worshipful Master and brethren, I find myself on my feet again for a brief response to your very kind toast. Let me reaffirm, brethren, what a pleasure it is for me to be in your midst at your meetings. I have always appreciated your warm welcome and the courtesies extended to me.

Having been with you now for a reasonable period of time, I can feel the friendship of each one of you. I trust that you feel the same way and that you have the confidence and trust to approach me frankly on matters of concern with which you feel I may be able to assist. Brethren, I have been around a long time, and can honestly say that the older I get, the better I used to be . . . on the other hand, age is only important if you are a bottle of wine!

Whilst I have no formal communications from Grand Lodge, I would like to attract your attention to some matters of importance. (*Here insert appropriate Grand Lodge official business items.*)

Brethren, it is a pleasure to be with you and I look forward with anticipation to our next happy meeting.

Thank you.

20. Worshipful Master

Response by the Worshipful Master

Brethren, thank you so much for your warm response to the toast. I cannot deny the upsurge of sentiment in me. The Past Masters amongst you will empathise with my emotions and to those yet to reach this exalted status of Worshipful Master of the lodge, all I can say is: prepare yourselves for an outstanding experience.

Brethren, in past years we have all enjoyed Installation ceremonies of the Masters who have gone before me. I have looked forwards, as I am sure many of you do, to the happy day when I would reach the chair of the lodge. Now, almost suddenly, here I am and all that I expected and hoped for has been exceeded by the wonderful atmosphere and your warm reception of me as your new Worshipful Master.

You know, brethren, deep, deep down . . . I am quite superficial! I do, however, look forward to the forthcoming year with great anticipation and a promise to fulfil all your expectations, which have led you to elect and install me as your Master. This will be an important year in my life and although I am not superstitious . . . I believe it is bad luck to be superstitious – all the omens are positive and everything is in place for me to serve you and the lodge to the best of my ability.

It is with pride that I will tread in the footsteps of the Past Masters who have preceded me and whom I have admired over the years. I hope to emulate their excellent work. I feel confident in the knowledge that I can call upon them any time for assistance and guidance. I know I will never stand alone . . . like the priest who addressed his congregation: 'If there is any one amongst you that wants to go to hell, please stand up.' One member did. 'Do you really want to go the hell?' enquired the priest. 'No,' replied the man, 'but I did not want you to be standing alone.'

Thank you again, brethren, and I promise to wield the gavel you entrusted me with – to make a noise to stop the noise – with respect and consideration.

Response by the Worshipful Master when a Past Master

Brethren, I cannot thank you enough for the warm sentiments you have expressed to me here, now this evening and your electing and installing me as your Master this afternoon. I promise you, brethren, that being a Past

Master detracts very little from the emotion of being installed into King Solomon's chair for a second time. I believe I will be able to use my experience to serve you and the lodge all the better.

There are some advantages, I feel, in reaching this exalted position for a second time. The sharpness of the lustre and excitement of the first occasion is not as intense. It therefore allows me to appreciate and enjoy with greater awareness my standing as your Master. Whilst I take pride to follow in the footsteps of distinguished Past Masters of this lodge, I also allow myself a view of the greater scope of Masonry Universal. It is a view that places me within the context of 350 years of history and 350 years of great men worldwide who chose Freemasonry as a vocation: Monarchs throughout Europe and our Kings of England; Presidents of the USA and so many men of letters and literature, politics and science *ad infinitum* . . . and you and me, brethren and many millions like us.

I have often wondered and asked what it was in Freemasonry that has been of such attraction to so many for so long. There has never been a determined answer and that may be the very secret of the success of our wonderful Craft: the fact that each of us discovers and derives his own satisfying fulfilment in the lodge room.

Brethren, I am indebted to you for electing and installing me as your Master and I will work diligently to fulfil all your expectations. Speaking of working diligently, a working stone mason was complaining about the low wages that he was being paid to which his employer replied: 'If you can consider being more operative with your work we will consider being more speculative with your pay!'

Thank you again, brethren for your warm sentiments.

21. Response by the Immediate Past Master or Installing Master

NOTE *The Immediate Past Master is NOT an Officer of the Lodge and in precedence he is immediately above the Chaplain i.e. Senior and Junior Wardens are senior to him.*

Worshipful Master and brethren, I have already had the pleasure of addressing you this evening when proposing the toast to the Master and I am grateful for this second opportunity to thank the Master for his very kind words and sentiments.

Last year was a memorable one for me because you all supported me so wholeheartedly. I know you will give the same support to our newly elected Master as I will, sitting on his left. I promise, Master, to do my very best to withhold my tongue until asked to speak! I can resist anything except for temptation . . . and the quality of our Master's ritual is such that I do not expect to be tempted.

Thank you again, Worshipful Master, for your kind sentiments. I am now honoured to be the most junior Past Master in the lodge and I will gladly and proudly support you and the lodge and look forward to sharing a happy year with you and the brethren of the lodge.

22. Response by the Master Elect

Worshipful Master and brethren, thank you for your kind and generous response to the Master's toast and it is with great anticipation and some trepidation that I look forward to the forthcoming year. I feel I am on the verge of reaching the peak of my Masonic career and have looked forward to this moment, that of being formally elected as your next Master, from the day of my appointment as a Steward in the lodge.

Brethren, over the years I enjoyed learning and reading about Freemasonry. I have always enjoyed reading, history especially. I will not forget the extent to which I felt my age when I realised that my children's history lessons at school were current affairs studies to me just yesterday and to what an extent history repeats itself . . . which is what I think is wrong with it. I have often found it curious that we have never actually defined history. Edward Gibbon unkindly stated that history is little more than the record of the crimes, follies and misfortunes of mankind and Emerson suggested that there is no actual history, it is all biography. It makes you think.

A year goes by quickly, brethren, and I will prepare myself for the task that will soon lie ahead of me. Meanwhile my full support for our Master will continue unabated.

In electing me, brethren, you have shown your confidence and I look forward to justifying your trust.

23. Response by The Initiate

Worshipful Master and brethren, my first duty is to thank my proposer Bro David Nixon and my seconder Bro Ralph Reader for introducing me to Freemasonry. I am particularly appreciative of their ensuring that I was initiated in this particular lodge where I was so happy to see smiling familiar faces, particularly when my sight was restored during the intriguing and fascinating ceremony.

It would be difficult and, I think, unwise of me to comment in any detail on this evening's proceedings. I can sincerely say, however, that my eyes have been opened, my curiosity aroused and I look forward with great anticipation to discover more in the future. Meanwhile I will do my best to serve this lodge so far as I can.

I would like to thank Bro Oliver Hardy for his kind toast to me and all the brethren of the lodge who participated in the ceremony that has now led me to be a very proud member of this lodge.

Thank you, Worshipful Master and brethren.

24. Response by an Honorary Member

Worshipful Master and brethren, you have given me great pleasure and pride by electing me an honorary member of this, my lodge of which I have been an active member for so many years. The circumstances leading to this very special privilege I now enjoy are known to you all and I am grateful for your recognising me in this way.

When I joined Freemasonry, I remember my proposer, Bro Thomas Lipton, saying to me 'Old Masons never die . . . but you'll have to join to find out why!' I now appreciate my Masonic life being extended in this very special manner.

My pride in being a member of the lodge has never waned over the past decades and it will now be strengthened by your gesture conveyed in such a special and most welcome manner. The other advice I was given by Bro Lipton was that 'a closed mouth gathers no foot' and I will therefore thank you, brethren and sit down.

25. Response by a Joining Member

Worshipful Master and brethren, I am absolutely delighted to be a member of your lodge and sincerely appreciate your electing me. I have been a regular visitor, as you well know, for some years and have had nothing but admiration for your warmth, brethren, and your work in lodge. It is, I feel, a true privilege for me now to be allowed to participate fully-fledged in lodge affairs. I am still a young man and feel I have much to offer.

The history of Freemasonry has long fascinated me and every meeting I attend I remain aware of the antiquity of our ritual and ceremonies. This very toast, and my response, are steeped in history. We can trace the earliest official records of Masonic toasting to our first *Book of Constitutions* published in 1723 which contains a collection of the Masons' songs at the end of the book. The Master's Song, (not to be confused with 'Here's to his health', which is of mid-Victorian origin) gives toasting instructions throughout, such as:

> *Stop here to drink the present Grand Master's health*
> *Stop here to drink to the glorious Memory of Emperors, Kings, Princes, Nobles, Gentry, Clergy, and learned Scholars, that ever propagated the Art*
> *Stop here to drink to the happy Memory of all the Revivers of the ancient Augustan Stile*

...and so forth.

In the 1738 second edition of our *Constitutions*, James Anderson stated that it was Dr. John T. Desaguliers, at his

Installation as the third Grand Master of the Grand Lodge of England, on 24 June 1719, that he '...forthwith reviv'd the old regular and peculiar Toasts or Healths of the Free Masons.' So we do follow in truly old and established traditions.

I would like to end, Worshipful Master and brethren, with the sentiments expressed in the last song in the 1723 *Constitutions* titled 'Enter'd Prentice's Song' which contains the famous lines:

> 'Let's Drink,
> Laugh and Sing,
> our Wine has a Spring,
> 'tis a Health to an Accepted Mason'.

Thank you again, brethren, for accepting me in your midst.

26. Visitors

Response by Visitors and Guests

Worshipful Master and brethren, thank you, Worshipful Master, for asking me to respond to this toast and I remain aware that I do so on behalf of the many guests present. I am confident that they would all wish me to convey to you and members of the lodge our heartfelt appreciation for a splendid afternoon and the sumptuous dinner we have enjoyed here at the festive board.

Visiting a lodge for me, brethren, has frequently been a wonderful escape from the stress and frustration of everyday life, especially at the present time when so many problems seem to engulf the business world in particular. I have been successful because I have kept things simple. I never use accountants, advisors, calculations and projections – I work on a simple principle of a ten per cent margin. I buy for ten and sell for a hundred. The principle of success is honesty. Can honesty be relative? At my gym shower room a few days ago a mobile phone on the bench rang. One of the athletes in the room picked it up and said, 'Yes? Hello, darling. £20,000 for a diamond ring? Well, if you are sure it is genuine and the jeweller is honest, buy it, darling.' He continued: '£35,000 for a new Mercedes sounds a good price to me, sweetheart. Buy it. Use my credit card.' He finished with, 'Bye sweetie pie.' He switched off the mobile phone, held it in the air and called out, 'Whose mobile is this?'

Brethren, visiting remains the essence for the success of Freemasonry. We have sadly gone past the early days when there was no need for particular security and any brother could turn up at any lodge meeting and be welcomed. It was the spurious publications after the 1730s that necessitated the introduction of attendance books and personal knowledge of a brother before admission. Rather interestingly, those early books remain our only source today for knowledge of early ritual among our forefathers. Ironically, even in those days it was not the disclosure of secrets that concerned Grand Lodge, but the fact that those unauthorised who may gain access to a lodge could also take improper advantage of the brethren's charity and charity at the time, as it is today, was the pivot around which Freemasonry rotated.

Worshipful Master and brethren, you have been delightful hosts to us. Your work in the Temple was exemplary, your hospitality at the festive board second to none and we thank you as we all look forward to the next occasion that we meet.

Response by Visitor and Guest (on a special occasion)

Worshipful Master and brethren, it is a particular privilege to be asked to respond to this toast to your guests on this very special occasion. We are delighted to have this privilege of sharing with you the celebration.

We do belong to an extraordinary institution, would you not agree, brethren? We are spread across the four quarters of the globe and every Mason, no matter what his creed, religion or nationality has the same sentiments embedded in his heart. It is not a wonder that on meeting a Mason for the first time, anywhere in the world, the genuine tenets of our Craft surface straight away. We feel immediate friendship and brotherhood, as if genuine members of a world family.

A sign outside a lodge room in Maryland, which I visited, is a perfect example. It stated: 'There are no strangers here – you are among friends you have not yet met.'

Lodge visiting, brethren, is the most overt manifestation of the benevolence of the heart. We should remember not to waste or take undue advantage of it. A Masonic friend of mine discovered, before a job interview, that his potential boss to be was a Freemason. He decided to test the advantages he may be able to derive as a young Mason. He wore Masonic cufflinks and tie and throughout the interview he made blatant Masonic references. Finally his boss asked 'If I offer you this position, what do you expect as a salary?' '£40,000 a year and six weeks holiday,' ventured the optimistic youngster. To which the boss replied, 'Halve it, and you begin!'

Thank you again Worshipful Master and brethren for allowing us to partake in your festivities on this exceptional afternoon in lodge and wonderful hospitality here at the festive board.

You have been delightful hosts. We thank you and wish your lodge continued success and happiness for many years, till time shall be no more.

Response by Visiting Speaker

Worshipful Master and brethren, your kind invitation to address you in this lodge and the very generous toast proposed to me by Bro Samuel Wesley, here at your excellent festive board, are much appreciated. Your wine has been excellent and your food plentiful. I admit I am not a big eater. I purchased a pizza yesterday and when asked whether I wanted it in four or six pieces, I responded instinctively: 'Four will be plenty, I don't think I could manage six pieces.'

You have heard quite a lot from me this afternoon and I do genuinely believe that modesty and brevity are the true secrets of a speaker's success. I learnt that lesson in practice when preparing for one of my lectures. I was in a truly upbeat mood; feeling good and very confident, even in a self centred mood. I looked at myself in the cloakroom mirror with satisfaction, gave my cheeks a little pinch to heighten the colour, adjusted my bow tie and as I was about to leave to make my way to the auditorium, I asked the attendant who had been observing me: 'How many really important people do you think there are in the audience this evening?' He replied without hesitation, 'One less than you think.'

Brethren, with that incident in mind, I will again thank you for the kind attention you gave me and for your warm and friendly hospitality.

27. Response for The Ladies
(normally by the President's Lady)

Mr President (my darling husband!), brethren, Ladies and Gentlemen, this has been an emotional and very enjoyable evening for me and, I have no doubt, for all the ladies present. It is always a delight to see our loved ones, especially those as close as a husband, reaching the pinnacle of his chosen vocation, be it a hobby or business. It is generous of you, brethren of the lodge, to keep to the custom of honouring your President's lady, in this instance his lifelong partner, with this toast so warm heartedly and ably delivered by Bro Walter Scott. Brethren, all the ladies present will agree with me that your hospitality has been exceptional and you have treated us with utmost courtesy and affection.

I would like to comment that a Mason's wife's lot is not always an easy one. Although I do not deny the freedom I enjoy when Wolfgang goes to Lodge; I don't have to cook dinner, I can spend time on the phone with my friends and watch whatever programme I want to on TV. It is great! Even on trips abroad when he took me with him – he visited the lodge and I went shopping. On the one occasion that I lost my credit card, he never reported it to the police. The thief was spending less money than I was.

It is, however, still a matter of finding that balance between freedom and responsibility that must be shared by husband and wife, friend and partner and it is a definite two-way thing. I have enjoyed sharing with Wolfgang his special year as Master of your lodge and his many years as a Freemason, because whilst I was happy to give him a free hand, I knew he never took advantage of that freedom and limited his Masonic activities to accommodate his family duties. I love him for that and I love you all brethren for allowing each other the fulfilment of your family duties whilst enjoying your Freemasonry to the utmost.

Thank you again for honouring us, your ladies, this evening.

28. Response by A Past Master o/b of Lodge
(by a senior member)

Brethren, it is my very good fortune to be the senior most member of the lodge on this occasion and by custom, I have the privilege of responding to the toast, ably and kindly addressed to us, Past Masters and Officers of the lodge, by Bro Benjamin.

In responding on behalf of the Officers, I speak collectively for the lodge. This includes the young stewards, aspiring for higher office, as well as the Past Masters, never resting on their laurels but assisting and working on for the lodge. If I may say so, as an insider, brethren, we have a great deal of talent in reserve and our future looks bright. We are surrounded by dedicated Masons. This dedication is reminiscent of the newly formed military platoon of Irish recruits, who when asked to get ready, aim and fire, dropped their guns and clapped three times three in unison.

We are now almost ten years old and our forthcoming anniversary will mark another landmark in the continued advancement and success, not just of this particular lodge but of Freemasonry as a whole.

I hope, brethren, you will take home with you memories of a memorable evening and remain aware of the small but important part we play in the development of the Craft as a whole. Thank you for the kind toast to the Past Masters and Officers of the lodge and your good wishes, brethren, are heartily reciprocated.

TOASTS WITHOUT RESPONSE

29. To Absent Brethren
(also known as the 9 O'clock Toast)

NOTE *Originally this toast was given as a charge after one of the lectures (Lect I Sc 3) which is now the Tyler's toast (see Appendix Item 41). 'Absent Brethren' are traditionally remembered at 9 o'clock, when the hands on the clock are on the square. In a number of lodges it is followed by an Ode which was originally a hymn by Isabella S. Stevenson entitled 'Holy Father in Thy Mercy' (Hymns Ancient and Modern No. 595) which was intended 'For absent Friends' and paraphrased to 'Absent Brethren'. The words are commonly sung to the hymn tune 'Cairnbrook' by Ebenezer Prout.*

Normally this toast is given as a simple statement by the Master without comment.

(The concept of silent fire practised in some lodges is a contradiction in terms.)

Brethren, I give you the 9 o'clock toast to absent brethren.

Followed by 'fire'

The following is the Stevenson Ode to 'Absent Brethren' recited in some Lodges:

Holy Father, in Thy mercy
Hear our anxious prayer,
Keep our loved ones, now far absent
'Neath Thy care

When in sorrow, when in danger
When in loneliness,
In Thy love look down and comfort
Their distress

Father, in Thy love and power
Architect Divine,
Bless them, guide them, save them, keep them,
They are Thine.
So mote it be.

Followed by 'fire'

30. Toast to a Departed Brother
(definitely without response)

Brethren, we cannot let this evening go by without remembering our late and much lamented Bro Anthony Trollope, who passed to the Grand Lodge above since our last meeting. Bro Anthony was a most active and loyal member of this lodge. He was friendly with a dry sense of humour and each one of us will miss his personable presence at our future meetings.

I would like to think, brethren, that Bro Trollope is even now watching us with the familiar wry smile on his face, feet dangling over a parapet, flanked by my dad on one side and by Winston Churchill on the other . . . Why not?

Brethren, I believe Bro Trollope died a happier man for having been a Freemason through his life and I now invite you to stand and drink Bro Trollope's departed memory.

Followed by 'fire'

31. Toast to a Brother on Recovery from Illness

Brethren, it is a delight to see back amongst us Bro Charles Dibdin, who has been sorely missed in the last few months, during his recent illness. We wish him excellent health and total recovery.

During his stay at Edgware Hospital, a call came through the switchboard to the head nurse asking: 'Is Mr Charles Dibdin in Ward 4F OK and recovered after his operation?' 'Yes, he is fine,' replied the nurse. 'When is he likely to be released from hospital?' asked the enquirer. 'He is due to be released Wednesday morning. Who is that speaking?' asked the nurse. 'This is Charles Dibdin in Ward 4F. The doctors won't tell me a thing!'

Bro Charles, we wish you good health and look forward to your company at our meetings for many years to come. I ask you all to stand and drink the good health of our Bro Charles Dibdin.
Followed by 'fire'

32. Toast to the Tyler and Organist
   (not to be confused with the Tyler's Toast)

Brethren, there are two brethren whose efforts on our behalf are often taken for granted. This may be because one, the Tyler, is placed outside the door of the lodge and the other, our Brother Organist, is hidden behind his instrument. They both, however, deserve our gratitude as they play such an important part, directly and indirectly, in all our ceremonies.

Our organist enhances our proceedings at every stage of

our ceremonies with his delightful music and deserves our appreciation and thanks. As for our Tyler, personally I will forever remain grateful to him. He inspired and instructed me as I spent hours in his company, whilst I was kept out of meetings I was unable to attend, as an enthusiastic apprentice and fellow craft. The Tyler is the first contact a candidate has with Freemasonry and his knowledge and enthusiasm are of paramount importance. Enthusiasm can be limited, though. On a chartered flight to New York we decided to hold a lodge meeting on board the plane but sadly had to give up as we could not find anyone to volunteer to act as the Tyler.

Brethren, please stand and join me in this toast to Brother Tyler and Brother Organist.

Followed by 'fire'

PRESENTATIONS

33. Membership (Grand Lodge) Certificate

NOTES *The membership Certificate is issued by the Grand Lodge and also referred to as the 'Grand Lodge Certificate'. It is presented to a brother in lodge after his attaining the third degree. There is no ritual dictated for this quasi-formal presentation although several suggestions are made in various ritual books. The following is an amended and much abbreviated version of the Emulation Lodge recommendation, allowing for your own adaptation of the necessary references to the significance of the document and the content of its design.*

Bro Israel Brodie, I have much pleasure in presenting you with your Grand Lodge certificate, to which you are now entitled, having attained the sublime degree of a Master Mason. The certificate, first introduced in 1819, is headed by the Arms of the present Grand Master and its design. Its content may be regarded as a simplified version of the First Degree Tracing Board, with which you will be familiar.

The three great pillars, Ionic, Doric and Corinthian, are said to support a Freemasons' lodge and are named Wisdom, Strength and Beauty, respectively and represent Solomon, King of Israel, Hiram King of Tyre and Hiram Abif. The pillars rest on the black and white chequered floor which represents Light and Darkness. The Celestial and Terrestrial Globes which you can see, point out Masonry Universal. There is also depicted the 'furniture of the Lodge', namely the Volume of the Sacred Law, the Square and Compasses. These are the three great and emblematical Lights of Freemasonry.

Other emblems shown are the 'Jewels', three movable – so named because they are worn by the Master and his Wardens and are transferable to their successors the Square, Level and Plumb Rule and three immovable Jewels, namely, the Tracing Board and the Rough and Perfect Ashlars. They are called 'immovable' because they lie open and immovable in the lodge. You will note that your year of Initiation into Freemasonry is shown as AL, *Anno Lucis*, or the year of Masonic Light, which precedes the Christian era by four thousand years. The seal of Grand Lodge has been impressed on it and the certificate is signed by the Grand Secretary.

Your certificate is a passport to regular Freemasonry, and you may be asked to produce it when visiting a lodge in a foreign constitution. Keep it handy with your regalia. It should not be framed or displayed.

Your certificate is not yet complete as it requires your usual signature in the place provided on the margin, and from which there should be no future variation. This you will now append at the Secretary's table.

34. Jewel Presentation

Anniversary Jewel

NOTE *The following is an amended format of the wording recommended by the Lodge of Emulation on the presentation of the 250th Anniversary Commemorative Jewel. The presentation would normally be made at the Installation of the new Master by the Installing Master, following the presentation of the Warrant, Book of Constitutions and By-Laws.*

Worshipful Master, earlier this afternoon, I had the pleasure and honour to invest you with the Collar and Jewel of your office as the newly installed Master of this Lodge. You will note that the collar, in addition to the Square, is also adorned with a Commemorative Jewel which embodies the central theme of the Arms first granted to the Masons Company of London in 1472.

The members of this Lodge, through 250 years of continued charitable activity, have played their part in the preservation and continuity of Freemasonry. This has also been done through the establishment of a special fund, the substantial income from which is placed at the disposal of the Royal College of Surgeons of England. It is intended to further research into the science of surgery as a real and practical contribution for the betterment of the health and happiness of humanity.

I feel sure, Worshipful Master, the members will always feel great pride and satisfaction at the fact that the adornment to the Master's Collar marks the Lodge's participation in this great enterprise.

Hall-Stone Jewel

NOTE *The following is an abbreviated and amended format of the wording recommended by the Lodge of Emulation for the presentation of the Hall Stone Jewel to the newly Installed Master, where applicable. The presentation would normally be made at the Installation of the new Master by the Installing Master when transferring the Hall-Stone Lodge Collaret and Jewel to his successor immediately before the investiture of officers.*

Worshipful Master, I present you with this, the Hall-Stone Jewel, which was conferred on this Lodge by the Most Worshipful Grand Master. You will observe that its form is symbolic with the dates 1914 and 1918 reminding us of the four years of supreme sacrifice. The winged figure in the centre represents Peace supporting a Temple. It symbolises the new Freemasons Hall, a gift of the English Craft, in memory of those brethren who made the supreme sacrifice for their King and country.

The Jewel is suspended by the Square and Compasses, two of the Great and Emblematical Lights in Freemasonry, and is attached to a ribbon, which I now place around your neck.

The wearing of this Hall-Stone Jewel by the Master of a lodge provides visible evidence that the lodge has faithfully discharged its obligations to the Fraternity and it should ever provide an inspiration to every brother to put service before self.

You will, in due course, transfer this Jewel to your successor and until then it should always be worn as part of your Masonic clothing. Your successor will, in turn, transfer it to his successor and so, it is to be hoped, it will ever adorn the Master of this lodge, until time with us shall be no more.

APPENDICES

35. Modes of Address: Masonic Ranks

NOTE *When addressing Masonic dignitaries present, those of the rank of 'Most Worshipful', 'Right Worshipful' and/or 'Very Worshipful' should be singled out after the 'Worshipful Master'. Clause 6 of our Book of Constitutions (outlined here) gives the details as well as the appropriate salutations:*

Titles, prefixes and abbreviations

6. The prefixes to be accorded to and used by brethren are as follows:

Most Worshipful (M.W.):
The Grand Master and Pro Grand Master, and Past Grand Masters and Past Pro Grand Masters.

Right Worshipful (R.W.):
Present and Past Deputy Grand Masters, Assistant Grand Masters, Provincial and District Grand Masters, Pro Provincial and District Grand Masters and Grand Wardens.

Very Worshipful (V.W.):
Present and Past Grand Chaplains, Presidents of the Board of General Purposes, Grand Registrars, Grand Secretaries, Presidents of the Board of Benevolence, Presidents of the Grand Charily, Presidents of the Masonic Foundation for the Aged and the Sick, Presidents of the Masonic Trust for Girls and Boys, Grand Directors of Ceremonies, Grand Sword Bearers, Grand Superintendents of Works and Grand Inspectors.

Provided always those members of the Grand Lodge who at the date of this amendment coming to operation (20 April 1969) held the offices of Grand Treasurer, or Past Grand Treasurer, Deputy Grand Registrar, or Past Deputy Grand Registrar shall continue to be described as 'Very Worshipful'.

Worshipful (W):
Other Grand Officers, present and past, and Masters of lodges, present and past. All other brethren shall have the style of 'brother' only.

36. Curious Toasts:

4 Crowned Martyrs

NOTES   *This is a special toast unique to the Quatuor Coronati Lodge 2076, the Premier Lodge of Masonic Research. It was created as a toast by the members at the beginning of the 20th century. It is given as an exchange between the Secretary and the Master, following the toast to the Worshipful Master and his response. Though it lapsed from time to time, the toast is still today celebrated at QC installation meetings:*

WM: Brother Secretary, on the feast of the Quatuor Coronati, whom do we honour?

Sec: Four craftsmen of old, Worshipful Master

WM: Why are these craftsmen deserving of honour?

Sec: Because at a time of religious persecution these craftsmen are said to have preferred death to the stain of falsehood and dishonour.

WM: Then brethren, let us drink in silence to honour the memory of the Quatuor Coronati.

Golden Eggs and Goldfinches

NOTES *This Masonic toast is to be found in the 1841 publication by C Daly in the relevant section of his book titled 'The Social and Convivial Toast-Master . . .' and is repeated by Spencer in 1877 in his 'Masonic Minstrel'. The definition of the slang 'Golden Eggs' is a reference to an expression of the period, long lost now, meaning 'One who has plenty of gold.' According to the Oxford English Dictionary (OED), the earliest non-Masonic source for this slang expression dates to 1603. A second similar expression is 'goldfinches' which again according to the OED may be defined as 'A gold coin, guinea, or sovereign' also tracing roots to 1602 and may be interpreted as meaning 'Great wealth to every Brother and golden guineas to our Lodges.'*

Cross Toasting

NOTES *This is a practice, now decried by Grand Lodge, where a brother at one end of the Dining Hall names and stands to drink the health of another some distance away. The problem with this 'cross' toasting is that it invariably gets out of hand because of the unruly system of just standing and shouting out a brother's name. In some instances it developed to the extent of the brethren standing on their chairs and even the table to have sight of the brother they are toasting. The effective 'ban' by the Grand Lodge is understandable.*

37. Masonic Fire

NOTE   *The origin of the fire dates to London records in 1686 when the newly elected Mayor visited each of the City Gates to make himself known to the local citizens and at each gate he gave a toast the King and the local populace. His personal guard accompanying him followed each toast by a volley of shots from their muskets. The earliest Masonic records are found in a French exposure of 1741, contemporaneously translated into English, giving us the routine for the 'fire' at the festive board. In early days the festive board is also where the ritual was carried out. The military connection is blatant throughout the process:*

Brethren present have a bottle of wine, each referred to as the 'barrell'. The wine is 'red powder' and 'white powder' is water. The goblets, now commonly known as firing glasses, are the 'cannon'. In the exposure, the brethren are invited to 'take powder', that is to fill their glasses with wine, followed by 'present arms'; i.e. raise your glasses, 'take aim', bring the filled glass to the mouth, and finally 'fire!' – drink. The exposure continues: *'All watching the Master all of the time and all being done in Military fashion with perfect disciplined unison.* [At the Master sign] *the Goblets, in perfect timing, are banged with force and noise on the table followed by 3 claps and 3 times the shout of Vivat! Vivat! Vivat!'* Or, in England, *'Huzza! Huzza! Huzza!'*

Terminology used today continues with the military nomenclature. The brethren are called upon t: 'charge' their glasses' followed by 'Good Fire'. Procedures relating to 'fire' are custom and not law. There are, therefore, no explicit rules. The tyling the dining room is to prevent non-Masons witnessing the P. . . L . . . R . . . gesture, which alludes to the first degree sign (it definitely is not the sign of the cross, nor is it a reference to the operative laying of cement for brick or stone work). Furthermore the idea that the Masonic 'fire' is somehow related or derived from the 21 gun salute given to royalty, is a fallacy. The custom of giving 'silent fire' in some lodges is a contradiction in terms.

38. Graces

Before Meals

NOTE *Grace is given before and after meals. In many lodges it is customary to sing Grace after the meal. The Grace that is sung (see b.3) is popularly headed 'For these and all Thy mercies' formally titled 'Laudi Spirituali'. It has been traced to a medieval melody: 'Alia Trinita Beata' in a manuscript collection of devotional music compiled by the 'Laudisti', an Italian religious fraternity based in Florence, dating to 1310.*

The standard Grace given is:

For what we are about to receive may the GAOTU give us grateful hearts and keep us ever mindful of the need of others

* * *

A small selection of other popular graces:

A Summer treat
A Feast to Eat
And kindly friends to make the day.

The best of Wine
From noble vines,
And a thirst to help us on the way.

So Lord, we thank thee for such grace,
And as we fill each tiny space
Help us ever bear in mind
Those to whom fortune's been less kind.

Thus praise and thanks and blessing mete
Which being done . . . good Lord, let's eat! *Amen*

* * *

Pa . . . Ta *Amen*

* * *

God bless us sinners
As we eat our Dinners. *Amen*

* * *

Some ha'e meat and can-na eat,
And some ha'e none that want it.
But we ha'e meat and we can eat,
And so the Lord be thank-et. *Amen*

Robert Burns

After Meals

The standard Grace after meals:

For what we have received may the GAOTU give us grateful hearts.

All respond 'Amen'

Another simple grace after meals:

For this refreshment of body and mind, we thank you O Lord, giver of all good things.

All respond 'Amen'

When Grace is sung the following are the 'Laudi Spirituali' words:

For these and all Thy mercies given
We bless and praise Thy name, O Lord.
May we receive them with thanks giving,
Ever trusting in Thy word.
To Thee alone be honour and glory,
Now and henceforth for ever more.

All respond 'Amen'

39. Toast List

NOTE *The current list in London for the Metropolitan Grand Lodge follows. Each Province will replace the appropriate names for their PGM and the equivalent Provincial Grand Officers.*

The Queen and the Craft

The Most Worshipful The Grand Master
His Royal Highness The Duke of Kent

The Most Worshipful Pro Grand Master
Peter Geoffrey Lowndes

The Right Worshipful Deputy Grand Master
Jonathan Spence

The Right Worshipful Assistant Grand Master
David Kenneth Williamson

And the rest of the Grand Officers, Present and Past

The Right Worshipful Metropolitan Grand Master
Russell John Race, DL.

The Deputy Metropolitan Grand Master
RW Bro Michael Ward PJGW

The Assistant Metropolitan Grand Masters

The Metropolitan Grand Inspectors.

The Officers of Metropolitan Grand Lodge.

Other holders of SLGR, LGR and LR
(and Officers of Provincial and District Grand Lodges,
Present and Past)

The Worshipful Master

The Immediate Past Master or Installing Master
(on installation night)

The Initiate or Initiates *(if any)*

The Visitors *(if any)*

The Tyler's Toast

40. Masonic Poems, Songs and Music

NOTE   *Freemasonry is rich with poetry and song easily to be found in Masonic literature. Masonic poems and songs go as far back as the earliest documents available to us. The Regius MS of c1390 is an 800 line poem that ends with the following modernised words:*

Amen! Amen!
So mote it be!
So say we all
for charity.
So mote it be.

Following is a very small and limited selection of Masonic songs and poetry.

a)   Enter'd 'Prentices Song

NOTE   *The earliest known Masonic song is the famous 'Enter'd 'Prentices Song' and the music, which appear in James Anderson's first Constitutions of 1723 with the comment: 'by our late Brother Mr Mathew Birkhead, deceas'd. To be sung when all grave business is over, and with the Master's leave.' It was first published as a single sheet of music in 1722. Both the words and music, adapted from an old Irish ballad, are attributed to the actor-singer and comedian, Mathew Birkhead (d. 1723). These are the words of the seven verses (verse VI and the Chorus have been added after 1723):*

I   Come let us prepare,
We Brothers that are
Assembled on merry occasion;
Let's drink, laugh, and sing:
Our wine has a Spring:
Here's a health to an Accepted Mason.

II   The world is in pain
Our secrets to gain,
And still let them wonder and gaze on;
They ne'er can divine
The Word or the Sign
Of a Free and an Accepted Mason.

III   'Tis this, and 'tis that,
They cannot tell what,
Why so many Great Men of the Nation
Should Aprons put on,
To make themselves one
With a Free and an Accepted Mason.

IV   Great Kings, Dukes, and Lords,
Have laid by their Swords,
Our myst'ry to put a good Grace on;
And ne'er been ashamed
To hear themselves named
With a Free and an Accepted Mason.

V   Antiquity's pride
We have on our side,
And it maketh men just in their station;
There's nought but what's good
To be understood
By a Free and an Accepted Mason.

VI We're true and sincere,
   And just to the Fair;
   They'll trust us on any occasion:
   No mortal can more
   The Ladies adore
   Than a Free and an Accepted Mason.

VII Then join Hand in Hand,
    To each other firm stand;
    Let's be merry, and put a bright face on:
    What Mortal can boast
    So Noble a Toast
    As a Free and an Accepted Mason.

Chorus
   No Mortal can boast So Noble a Toast
   As a Free and an Accepted Mason

b) *Robert Burns'*
   Address to the Haggis – a parody

NOTE *Bro. Robbie Burns (1759-1796) remains the most loved
      and honoured of all Scottish poets. Of his multitude of
      poems, several Masonic, the 'Address to the Haggis' is
      among the ones most often heard. It is recited at 'Burns
      Night' celebrated throughout the world as near 25
      January as possible, that being the poet's birthday. Here
      is an easily understood 'translation' parody by my great
      friend, Bro Bob Upton:*

Translation of the Traditional Speech to a Large Scottish
Sausage (*as near to the original as possible in meter and verse
or as the Great Bard might have written it today if he were
an Englishman!*)

Good luck to your appearance and shapely look
First choice of puddings, in every cookery book
You beat them all with your paunch, tripe and inners
Deserving a good long grace, from us poor sinners

This heavy plate, you more than fill
And a size, to equal a distant hill
Your skewers would help to mend a mill
if ever a need
Whilst through your skin, your juices distil
like a brown bead

See the countryman, clean his knife to please
And opens you up with skilful ease
Spreading your innards, as if to appease
The shape of a ditch
Then oh! what a wonderful tasty tease
warm, heady, rich

Then armed with spoons, all eat with gusto
Not wanting to be last, on they must go
Their stomachs are stretched with such a cargo
tight like a drum
Then older wise men rest, thrashing no ego
a thanks they hum

Is there anyone contemplating his French Ragout
Or vegetable soup to sicken a crew
Or a fricassee making one spew
with disgusting wish
Would look down with a sneering, scornful view
on such a dish

Poor devil, see him, with his worthless food
Making him feeble as any un-nurtured brood
His limbs for strength are being sued
Note, his minute fist
And as for action, he's little endued
he'll never be missed

But Note the countryman Haggis fed
The earth trembles beneath his tread
Held in his eager hand, a sword
which he'll make whistle
And legs and arms and heads will fall
like the tops of a thistle

You Gods, who, for all mankind care
Providing them with their bill of fare
No men want a skimping share
that slops in a dish
If you really want their grateful prayer
answer their wish:

Give them a HAGGIS

c)   *I Love to Love a Mason*

NOTE   *This is the text of a song from William K Ziegfeld's
        (1873-1927) 1910 musical called 'The Girl in the
        Kimono':*

1st Verse:
Sweetheart tell me true what is it Masons do
When they all get together in the Lodge?

Really I'm delirious; it's all so mysterious.
When I ask, you always seem to dodge.
Won't you put me hip
To the password and the grip
For to know them really must be fine.
I'll never tell a soul
And I'll gladly pay the toll
Now won't you please show me just one sign.

Chorus:
I love to love a Mason 'cause a Mason never tells
In joyful expectation of those tuneful wedding bells
Spooning honeymooning, as we love and kiss and squeeze;
Wooing, softly cooing become a Mason by degrees.

2nd Verse:
Honey I'll agree to work the first degree
But you must try your best to do your part.
I will whisper in our ear, so no one else will hear
The passwords "Darling of my heart".
The ring upon your hand
Is the sign you understand
That you will be forever true to me,
I'll kiss your ruby lips,
That's a Mason's fondest grip,
When I put you through the first degree.

d)   Master's Song

NOTES *The Master's Song (not to be confused with the 28
verse Master's Song in Anderson's Constitutions of
1723) consists of just three verses and is titled 'Here's
to his health in a song'. The words are by Brother*

Richard Rome Bealey (1828-1887) with the music composed, inter alia, by Brother Dr. John Morgan Bentley of Alexander Lodge No. 993. It was written between 1866 and 1868.

Verse I solo:
This world is so hard and so stony;
That if a man is to get through,
He'd need have the courage of Nelson,
And plenty of Job's patience too.
But a man who is kind to another
And cheerfully helps him along,
God Bless such a man and a brother.
And here's to his health in a song.
And here's to his health, here's to his health and here's to his health in a song.

Chorus:
And here's to his health,
Here's to his health
And here's to his health in a song.

Verse II;
This life is as cheerless as Winter,
To those who are cold in the heart;
but a man who is warm in his nature,
Bids Winter for ever depart
The ground that he treads on will blossom,
Till beauty around him shall throng;
God Bless such a man and a brother.
And here's to his health in a song.
And here's to his health; here's to his health
And here's to his health in a song.

Chorus

Verse III:
As clouds that in sunshine are open,
And silvered by light passing through;
So men who are generous in spirit,
Are blessed by the good deeds they do;
There's nothing like helping another
For getting one's own self along;
Who does this is truly a brother.
And here's to his health in a song.
And here's to his health; here's to his health
And here's to his health in a song.

All stand to sing chorus

e)   **Rudyard Kipling's** (1865-1936) '*My Mother-Lodge*' is
     the best known of his many Masonic poems:

There was Rundle, Station Master,
An' Beazeley of the Rail,
An' 'Ackman, Commissariat,
An' Donkin' o' the Jail;
An' Blake, Conductor-Sargent,
Our Master twice was 'e,
With 'im that kept the Europe-shop,
Old Framjee Eduljee.

Outside – 'Sergeant! Sir! Salute! Salaam!'
Inside – 'Brother,' an' it doesn't do no 'arm.
We met upon the Level an' we parted on the Square,
An' I was Junior Deacon in my Mother-Lodge out there!

We'd Bola Nath, Accountant,
An' Saul the Aden Jew,
An' Din Mohammed, draughtsman
Of the Survey Office too;
There was Babu Chuckerbutty,
An' Amir Singh the Sikh,
An' Castro from the fittin'-sheds,
The Roman Catholick!

We 'and't good regalia,
An' our Lodge was old an' bare,
But we knew the Ancient Landmarks,
An' we kep' 'em to a hair;
An' lookin' on it backwards
It often strikes me thus,
There ain't such things as infidels,
Excep', per'aps, it's us.

For monthly, after Labour,
We'd all sit down and smoke
(We dursn't give no banquits,
Lest a brother's caste were broke),
An' man on man got talkin'
Religion an' the rest,An' every man comparin'
Of the God 'e knew the best.

So man on man got talkin',
An' not a Brother stirred
Till mornin' waked the parrots
An' that dam' brain-fever-bird;
We'd say 'twas 'ighly curious,
An' we'd all ride 'ome to bed,
With Mo'ammed, God, an' Shiva
Changin' pickets in our 'ead.

Full oft on Guv'ment service
This rovin' foot 'ath pressed,
An' bore fraternal greetin's
To the Lodges east an' west,
Accordin' as commanded
From Kohat to Singapore,
But I wish that I might see them
In my Mother-Lodge once more!

I wish that I might see them,
My brethren black an' brown,
With the trichies smellin' pleasant
An' the hog-darn passin' down;
An' the old khansamah snorin'
On the bottle-khana floor,
Like a Master in good standing
With my Mother-Lodge once more.

Outside – 'Sergeant! Sir! Salute! Salaam!'
Inside – 'Brother,' an' it doesn't do no 'arm.
We met upon the Level an' we parted on the Square,
An' I was Junior Deacon in my Mother-lodge out there!

41. Tyler's Toasts

NOTES *The Tyler's Toast concludes the after-proceedings of the*
Masonic banquet. The Worshipful Master calls for the
Tyler with two rapid knocks of the gavel. The Tyler
stands behind the Worshipful Master, often with his
left hand on the Master's shoulder and a glass of wine
in his right hand. The Tyler is not always present at
dinner and any brother may be invited to give this
last and symbolic toast.

The standard time-honoured toast is:

Brethren, by command of the Worshipful Master I give
    you the Tyler's Toast:

To all poor and distressed Freemasons
wherever scattered over the face of land or sea;
wishing them a speedy relief from all their sufferings
and a safe return to their native land if they so desire.

*The Brethren rise and drink to the Toast and the Tyler leads
the 'Fire'.*

This is the Translation of the Russian Tyler's toast:

Brethren, according to ancient custom among
    Freemasons,
Before rising from the festive board,
Let us turn our thoughts to those of our brethren
Who are scattered over the face of the earth.
Let us wish solace to those who suffer;
    A speedy recovery to those in sickness;
An improvement in their lot to those in misfortune;
Humility to the fortunate;
    And to those who stand before the Gates of Death:
    Firmness of Heart and Peace in the Eternal East.

ACKNOWLEDGEMENTS AND BIBLIOGRAPHY

My thanks are extended to numerous brethren of whom Martin Faulks, the unsung hero who has brought to light dozens and dozens of Masonic literary works, is the only one I will mention. As has now become customary, I have used many Internet sources, here generally acknowledged and I have made liberal use of AQC, the transactions of Quatuor Coronati Lodge of Research No. 2076, the Premier Lodge of Masonic Research in the world. The following are additional specific sources:

Beresiner, Yasha. *Masonically Speaking.*
    Lewis, Surrey 2008

Buchanan, Peter. *Masonic Gags and Gavels.*
    Lewis, Surrey 1980

Carr, Harry. *The Freemason at Work.*
    QCCC, London 1977

Carr, Harry. *Queries* AQC **82**: 3328

Hamill, John (NOTES) Country Stewards' (Green
    Apron). AQC **89**: 223

Hamill, J M. *Vocal Music in Craft Ceremonies.*
    AQC **88**: 187-9

Monkhouse, Bob *Just Say A Few Words*
    Lennard, Beds 1988

Smyth, Frederick. *A Reference Book for Freemasons.*
    QCCC, London 1998